East Asian Popular Culture

Series Editors
Yasue Kuwahara
Department of Communication
Northern Kentucky University
Highland Heights, KY, USA

John A. Lent
International Journal of Comic Art
Drexel Hill, PA, USA

This series focuses on the study of popular culture in East Asia (referring to China, Hong Kong, Japan, Mongolia, North Korea, South Korea, and Taiwan) in order to meet a growing interest in the subject among students as well as scholars of various disciplines. The series examines cultural production in East Asian countries, both individually and collectively, as its popularity extends beyond the region. It continues the scholarly discourse on the recent prominence of East Asian popular culture as well as the give and take between Eastern and Western cultures.

Gemma Ballard

Urban Landscapes and National Visions in Post-Millennial South Korean Cinema

From Seoul to Soul

Gemma Ballard
School of East Asian Studies
University of Sheffield
Sheffield, UK

ISSN 2634-5935   ISSN 2634-5943 (electronic)
East Asian Popular Culture
ISBN 978-3-031-29738-0   ISBN 978-3-031-29739-7 (eBook)
https://doi.org/10.1007/978-3-031-29739-7

© The Editor(s) (if applicable) and The Author(s), under exclusive licence to Springer Nature Switzerland AG 2023
This work is subject to copyright. All rights are solely and exclusively licensed by the Publisher, whether the whole or part of the material is concerned, specifically the rights of translation, reprinting, reuse of illustrations, recitation, broadcasting, reproduction on microfilms or in any other physical way, and transmission or information storage and retrieval, electronic adaptation, computer software, or by similar or dissimilar methodology now known or hereafter developed.
The use of general descriptive names, registered names, trademarks, service marks, etc. in this publication does not imply, even in the absence of a specific statement, that such names are exempt from the relevant protective laws and regulations and therefore free for general use.
The publisher, the authors, and the editors are safe to assume that the advice and information in this book are believed to be true and accurate at the date of publication. Neither the publisher nor the authors or the editors give a warranty, expressed or implied, with respect to the material contained herein or for any errors or omissions that may have been made. The publisher remains neutral with regard to jurisdictional claims in published maps and institutional affiliations.

Cover illustration: Gw. Nam/Getty Images

This Palgrave Macmillan imprint is published by the registered company Springer Nature Switzerland AG.
The registered company address is: Gewerbestrasse 11, 6330 Cham, Switzerland

Acknowledgements

I would like to thank the following people, without whom I would not have been able to complete this book:
    First and foremost, Professor Jonathan Rayner, for his continued guidance, cherished support and steadfast encouragement.
    Professor Kate Taylor-Jones, for her invaluable advice and kind leadership.
    My editors Camille Davies, Professor Yasue Kuwahara and the brilliant team at Palgrave Macmillan for taking a chance on my work and helping me navigate the publication process.
    Professor Frances Gateward, for making me believe that my research was worthy of publication.
    My very good friends Sarah Evans Alwin and Dr Kyuin Kim, for their constant reassurance and treasured companionship.
    My teacher and friend, Mr Tenniswood—for starting it all!
    And finally, my wonderful family, for their patience, understanding and, above all else, their unwavering love and support.
    I would especially like to thank my Mum, who has been, and continues to be, the biggest blessing in my life.

About the Book

The urban landscape appears symbolically, socially and culturally integral to contemporary South Korean film, to such an extent that it can be considered as a constitutive element of the country's national cinematic identity. While the inherently intertextual and heteroglossic nature of the cityscape captures the increasingly postmodern and self-conscious nature of many national cinemas, South Korean film seems to take this notion ostensibly further, often positing Seoul as a purely cinematic, impressionistic and hybridised construct, upon which the definitions of character, narrative and genre are heavily reliant. However, even though a level of celluloid artifice is always apparent in this presentation, the capital city is still rendered (on screen and in many other forms of South Korean popular culture) as an authentic and localised space, integral to national consciousness. Using five different approaches to urban space, from five different perspectives, this study seeks to understand why Seoul remains important to the preservation and recognition of the South Korean film industry as an independent, autonomous and nationally unique institution.

While all chapters and their critical approaches are thematically linked, they each function as pivotal case studies and are grounded in close textual analysis of a recent and relevant South Korean film. The book posits that a *nationally* focused approach is instrumental to our understanding of world cinema texts and therefore identifies the critical and potential issues that arise when relying on the *transnational*—which, in this particular instance, is rendered as an overly fluid theoretical framework that diminishes cultural specificity. A concentration on the national produces and contextualises a nationally specific and relevant text, which is paramount to our understanding of how South Korean cinema operates on the global stage, as well as on a purely domestic level. Fundamentally, this book argues that it remains crucial to 'nationalise' film, to read film textually, nationally and generically, and to identify the unique cultural, social and historical signifiers that, collectively, contribute to a country's cinematic identity and character.

Contents

1 Introduction 1
2 The Psycho-geographical City 13
3 The Generic City 43
4 The Hyper-masculine City 73
5 The Suppressive City 109
6 The Oppositional City 141
7 Conclusion 159

Filmography 167
Index 169

About the Author

Gemma Ballard currently works in the School of East Asian Studies (SEAS) at the University of Sheffield, UK. Her research background is in Film Studies and Film Theory. She is particularly interested in discussions around national and transnational cinemas, cinematic landscapes, genre theory and narratives of postmodernity. In 2021 and 2022, she presented her work at the prestigious International South Korean Women's Cinema Conference and the Sheffield Centre for Research in Film (SCRIF). In her spare time, Gemma can be found enjoying time with her family, baking, reading a Scandinavian crime novel or watching reruns of *Frasier*.

CHAPTER 1

Introduction

It is no exaggeration to say that South Korean cinema is facing a critical turning point. These are exciting and interesting times for a national film industry that, up until the 1990s, had faced several periods of decline, numerous exterior threats and sustained levels of economic instability. Now, however, the outlook is considerably more optimistic, and we are rightly starting to reconsider how we situate South Korean cinema, along with its key directors, producers, script writers and audiences, within both the global sphere of popular film culture and the more theoretical parameters of cinema consumption. In 2020, acclaimed director Bong Joon Ho's latest film *Parasite* (2019/2020), a satirical tale about class division, family relationships and the urban experience, was nominated in the 'Best Picture' category at the 92nd Annual Academy Awards ceremony. It ultimately went on to win the award—the first foreign language film to do so (BBC 2020).

The fact that it was nominated for 'Best Picture' (in addition to 'Film Not in the English Language') suggests that a notable shift is taking place. Whether the Oscars are still relevant, important or, indeed, fair is a debate that is increasingly explored and contested within the wider film community. In recent years, the ceremony and the institutions that surround it have faced numerous controversies, the majority of which have largely revolved around a continued lack of diversity (with regards to the systemic

© The Author(s), under exclusive license to Springer Nature Switzerland AG 2023
G. Ballard, *Urban Landscapes and National Visions in Post-Millennial South Korean Cinema*, East Asian Popular Culture,
https://doi.org/10.1007/978-3-031-29739-7_1

under-representation and marginalisation of ethnic minority groups) and the failure to recognise female directors, writers and producers within the industry. However, one must acknowledge that, even in the face of such issues, *Parasite's* recognition and success at the Oscars (as well as at many other international film festivals) signifies an important and long-awaited step forward for the Korean film industry as a leading, national institution. For almost 30 years, the South Korean government has been investing a substantial amount of money into its key entertainment markets: music, television and film. This support has sustained what is now commonly and widely known as 'Hallyu', or the 'Korean Wave'—a 'phenomenon of cultural production that has been used to promote Korean interests overseas' (Walsh 2014, p. 13). Evidently, the Hallyu formula is working well. *Parasite's* win acts not only as a celebration of South Korean cinema specifically, but it more importantly demonstrates how Korean national culture has finally found its place on a *global* stage.

Nevertheless, it is still possible to be partially cynical about the film's numerous achievements. As Cho Hae Joang observes, 'when a South Korean movie wins a prize in a Western film festival, this attests either to the country's expanding national strength or to the enduring strength of orientalism' (Cho 2002, p. 150). While it may be fair to argue that some of *Parasite's* success on the international film circuit is a reflection and/or extension of archaic attitudes towards the East (in that it potentially satisfies orientalist perspectives and the West's superficial desire to experience a level of 'othered', cultural spectacle), one must take into account the sense of cinematic history embedded within the film, the career trajectory of its director and the incremental rise of the Hallyu movement since the beginning of the Twenty-first century. To place such strong emphasis on the Western reception of and response to the film is to undermine its national authority and relevance completely. This approach also disregards South Korea's profound cultural and economic growth. Fundamentally, *Parasite's* journey to the screen and its eventual commercial and critical dominance cannot be considered as a mere 'moment' for the Korean film industry—that is a fleeting, novel or, indeed, inconsequential happening. On the contrary, the film acts as a crowning, cinematic step for the domestic industry and an amalgamation and focusing of all the stylistic characteristics that have defined South Korean cinema in the post-millennial age.

The successes of films such as *Shiri* (1999), *Oldboy* (2003) and the recent *Train to Busan* (2016), alongside countless other smaller budget films such as *Oasis* (2002), *Paju* (2009) and *Burning* (2018), have, collectively, contributed to the steady yet assured growth of South Korean cinema. With every new release and entry into a prominent film festival, there has been an increasing level of attention given towards the movement of the institution as a whole and, more importantly, a rise in admiration for its often idiosyncratic and culturally unique, yet globally accessible, productions. 'Hybrid' and 'self-aware' are terms often used to characterise the cinematic endeavours of South Korea, and for entirely understandable reasons. The industry has closely examined, analysed and sought to incorporate major film discourses, styles and movements into its own, *nationally exclusive* template, be it in its approach to production, distribution or exhibition. The forging of this textual and institutional dialogue has allowed the industry to create a space in which to generate stronger, and ultimately more competitive, cinematic narratives.

Thus, the creation of a film like *Parasite* functions as part of a natural, expected and inevitable stage in South Korean cinema's overall development. More significantly, the film must be viewed as an extension of its director—a prominent Korean auteur that, over the past 20 years, has greatly contributed to the cinematic landscape of his homeland and helped to solidify the aforementioned dominance of the domestic film industry. Certain aspects of Bong's previous films, whether of a stylistic, symbolic or textual nature, can all be identified, on some level, within *Parasite*. From elements of genre-bending to the now familiar hints of anti-American sentiment, the marks of the auteur's distinctive, nationalised aesthetic are evident and, in some cases, heightened. Together with the movement of the industry in its entirety (a now viable commercial export) and Bong Joon Ho's expanding directorial profile, the profound response to *Parasite* is indicative of the South Korean film industry's determination to create and ultimately sustain its own cinematic authority and autonomy.

Collectively, all these different factors have created a sense of momentum, from both a domestic and international viewpoint, and this momentum has provided a foundation upon which a cinematic renaissance period, or a new 'Golden Era' of South Korean filmmaking, can continue to flourish and expand. Therefore, in response to Cho Hae Joang's previous argument, one must acknowledge that *Parasite's* success and, indeed, the success of the institution from which it hails, is a reflection of South Korea's 'expanding national strength', and its determination to cultivate a coherent, self-governed and independent cultural identity (Cho 2002, p. 150). The key question to consider now, especially in the *post-Parasite* era, is to what exact extent we should continue to read South Korean cinema in terms of

- its historical and formal relationship to other national cinemas;
- its debts and divergences from precedents within the national film industry;
- its relationship with the global film categories, genres or stereotypes that condition the wider viewer responses to it.

While it may be impossible to completely abandon the comparative approach that has often been used to analyse the 'state' of South Korean cinema and, indeed, the position of other national cinemas, it is now more important than ever to recognise the structural dangers and limitations this act perpetuates.

An Exclusive Club: Issues with the 'East Asian' Paradigm

Upon reading or hearing the term 'East Asian Cinema', it is most often the case that the films of Japan, China and Hong Kong form a principal collective canon and therefore receive a greater level of critical attention. They appear to maintain stylistic and thematic precedence, most likely because it has become a normalised endeavour to compare and contrast their narratives and production styles against those embedded within the American film system. This is to be expected, given that all these national cinemas have long since established their own formal and commercial platform. In contrast, the South Korean film industry is still considered as a fairly 'new' cultural outlet, as it didn't acquire full economic and commercial stability until the 1990s. Even though the development during this period was swift and substantial, Dooboo Shim notes how '*The Oxford History of World Cinema*, published in 1996 … covered every aspect of international filmmaking', but did not 'make any reference to Korean cinema' (Shim 2016, p. 25). Arguably, omissions and oversights such as this have, up until recently, shaped the global impression of Korean national filmmaking (all while it has simultaneously solidified its own success on a domestic scale).

As a result, South Korean cinema has remained somewhat of a cinematic, cultural and even geographical anomaly, constantly oscillating in the purgatorial space between its renowned Asian neighbours and the dominant voice of Hollywood. While the latter stands as a singular and isolated industry from a purely geographical perspective (Hollywood releases are, to a large extent, classed as 'American' productions), the term 'East Asian Cinema' ignites a much more complex readerly issue because it homogenises a number of separate, distinctive (and thus, competing) countries, spaces, identities and/or societies. Despite the textual dilemmas that this comparative act introduces, namely generalisation and simplification, the aforementioned canon has been created, and we now have a fairly concrete idea of what to expect from the film industries that jointly contribute towards the 'East Asian' paradigm. This ostensibly 'solid' knowledge is the result of a collective desire to understand and further categorise the growing levels of cultural production in the dominant spaces of Japan, China and Hong Kong. This desire, however, and the place from which it is born, are indicative of a troublesome ambition to govern the image of, and the response to, East Asian texts. As previously mentioned, readings of East Asian popular culture have largely been informed by a persistent and underlying sense of difference or 'otherness'—that is a culmination of ideas born largely from Western interpretation. If Hollywood cinema represents the conventional, even the 'normalised', it is commonly assumed that other world cinemas, particularly those from East Asia, appear the opposite of this. A process of sustained differentiation is not only deeply ingrained within these constructions, but it is also relied upon to create filters, and thus establish key signifiers, through which we can read certain texts.

This perspective is, of course, highly problematic and, now more than ever, occasionally inaccurate and easily challenged. While the stylistic, cultural and tonal differences still persist (and necessarily so), the film industries of the East have arguably as much awareness of popular discourse and genre as their dominant Western counterpart. We now, for example, have a stronger awareness of the history and development of these industries individually and are therefore able to identify the ways in which they have engaged with, inherited and utilised aspects of commercial filmmaking (while simultaneously manifesting their own unique approach to, and creation of, new genres, narratives, etc). Of course, globalisation is key to this process. Communication is growing, technology is expanding and dominant forms of modern popular culture seem to continuously overlap, merge and 'borrow' certain imagery from one another—the structural makeup of *Parasite*, as a more popular and recent example, attests to this (yet it is still rightly considered as an unequivocally Korean text). The film clearly engages with transparent genre patterns (elements of black comedy, the thriller and horror, for example), which function as a means to heighten the general accessibility of the piece. Indeed, many Korean films of the post-millennial era operate in a similar way and can, in some capacity, be read as clear genre texts.

One must therefore acknowledge that the dividing line of distinction between the East and West (purely with regard to commercial practice) grows ever more tenuous, most likely as a result of increased transnational endeavour, modernisation and self-awareness in and amongst these industries. This is not to say that clear comparisons cannot be identified, only that the manner in which they are located involves a certain level of structural rigidity and may therefore appear outdated. There are notable inconsistencies, for example, not only in the readings of national cinemas (and what constitutes a country's national cinematic identity) but also in our understanding of genre and narrative, especially where popular and mass-consumed film is concerned. The idea of national cinema in particular has, in recent years, been criticised for evoking, as Jung Bong Choi describes, 'a parochial and invidious mindset' and can thus be viewed as a fairly archaic practice (Choi 2011, p. 174). It can certainly be argued that the established readings of, and attitudes towards, the concept of national cinema are riddled with a number of paradoxes, contradictions and limitations. One might question, for example, if it is possible to concretely define a national cinematic identity when 'nationhood' itself is now considered to be an ambivalent and somewhat antiquated term (that often spurs negative, jingoistic connotations). Furthermore, how might we explain what South Korean cinema is, without confidently knowing what constitutes 'Korean-ness'? And is this something we should be actively pursuing at all?

The answer may lie in a fundamental *recognition* of national cinema, as opposed to a sustained *reliance* on it (and the same might be said for genre, narrative and a broader sense of film discourse when considered alongside global film landscapes). As Choi further observes, 'one must not overlook the significance of *nationalising* cinemas—that is, making conscious efforts to morph cinematic characters for a nation' (Choi 2011, p. 180). Ultimately, I would suggest that it is still highly necessary to associate a country or nation with a specific kind of film identity and autonomous style. In order to do this, we must recognise the academic value and credibility of 'national cinema', as both a helpful critical filter and theoretical approach. The act of locating cultural, social and stylistic identifiers remains integral to the formation of cinematic character and allows us to positively differentiate one world industry from another. A nationally focused reading (with a clear intent to identify and isolate unique national tropes) can produce a nationally significant text. This active and engaged method is needed to sustain the positive and distinctive qualities that, collectively, contribute towards the filmic landscape of a particular nation state. Therefore, it is not the 'national' concept that remains problematic, only our [previous] approach towards it and the connotations formerly linked to it—namely the idea of ownership and exclusivity.

For many reasons (some of which are to be explored within this book), South Korean cinema cannot, and perhaps should not, be read as part of the 'East Asian' model, nor should it be forever compared to Hollywood endeavour. All of which indicates that, as a fair alternative, the industry must now be acknowledged as a distinctive, unique and independent national cinema. This pivotal reconsideration of how we approach such texts provides us with the space to further examine the idiosyncratic tendencies of 'new' Korean film and its ability to reimagine generic film tropes in a manner that is culturally and, above all else, nationally unique. To what degree South Korean cinema remains separate, however, remains an ambivalent issue, particularly because its current situation is evolving so rapidly. One also has to take into account the industry's complex history and its continued impact on contemporary cultural production. It seems that, now more than ever before, South Korean popular culture is occupying a dominant space in global media consciousness, and as such, we must examine its development on a much larger, historiographical scale, in order to better understand *how* and *why* it has reached this successful stage.

PLACE, SPACE AND THE URBAN LANDSCAPE: IDENTIFYING THE COMPARATIVE BOUNDARIES OF SOUTH KOREAN FILM

Fundamentally, South Korea's position amongst the current canon of prominent East Asian cinema is somewhat difficult to locate and place, largely due to a sense of relentless movement and expansion with regard to national identity and how such is rendered within wider popular culture (and this may also extend to its productions in television and music). Similar to the occasionally presumptuous comparisons made between

Korea and Hollywood, it is equally problematic to align the former alongside its much closer global neighbours, though this is often the case. There is always the potential danger of further homogenising these regions when we place their key cultural institutions under the umbrella term of 'East Asia'. In the context of film studies, there are notable differences not only in the growth and development of these world cinemas but also in the very societies that they aim to portray and ultimately engage with. This means that despite their physical proximity, and perhaps even despite their complex historical and social relation to one another, they now stand as independent cultural discourses and should therefore be read as such.

Where there is a degree of tonal and stylistic stability in the film industries of Japan, Hong Kong and China (perhaps because they have all long since secured critical and commercial acknowledgement), in South Korea there appears to be a persistent investigative agenda, most likely as a result of its own turbulent history. From the Golden Age of the 1950s and 1960s, the eventual decline of the 1970s, and through to the current Renaissance, South Korean cinema has not had the easiest of journeys. The timeline of the national film industry has been marked, conditioned and characterised by a number of social, political and cultural events that have taken place throughout the Twenty-first century. The landscape of South Korea has changed dramatically in a short space of time, and for better or worse, the film industry has been forced to adapt to, acknowledge and, in some cases, survive such changes. This is yet another reason why we should read Korean cinema in terms of the *national*, as opposed to the *transnational*. The vast transformations in Korean film texts, as well as the very infrastructure of the film industry itself, are a direct reflection of the seismic shifts embedded within a country that has oscillated between periods of stability and instability.

Ultimately, South Korean society has changed—and so too has South Korean cinema.

Yet, what has remained consistent in South Korean film throughout these profound historical junctures is a continued focus on the cityscape or, more specifically, Seoul, and the various ideologies embedded within urban life. Oh Youjeong takes this further and argues that there is now an emphatic 'alliance between cultural production [in South Korea] and urban policies', and this alliance exists in response to growing media interest and evolving domestic strategy (Oh 2021, p. 2). From the post-colonial and post-liberation space to the present day, the capital city of South Korea has manifested a gravitational force, securing the attention of both the national and international gaze. This has been, in large part, due to the over-centralisation of Seoul, whether it be within the national consciousness of South Korea or as a curious fixture of global scrutiny.

There are certain national enquiries that are still acutely connected to South Korea—questions concerned with the present 'state' of the capital city, its complex identity and, by extension, the identities of the people who exist within it. Seoul has thus become a social, historical and political microcosm—a canvas upon which the wider movements, transitions and developments of a national society can be unveiled and better understood. To utilise Seoul as an investigative tool (cinematically or otherwise) is indicative of the domestic desire to further explore and ultimately take control of the dominant image of South Korean identity. One must consider, for instance, the contained impact of the country's own 'interior' history, as well as the lengthy process of finding and negotiating an independent voice throughout sustained periods of national trauma (the effects of which are still present today). South Korea's collective character has had to simultaneously contend and cooperate with two exterior forces, Japan and America, and this undertaking has undoubtedly ingratiated itself into all aspects of social and cultural development, through to the present day.

South Korea's film industry began, as Frances Gateward observes, 'as one of the most stifled, hindered by the annexation of the peninsula of Japan ... and the fragmentation of the nation [during] the civil war' (Gateward 2007, p. 4). While this former tension no longer presents itself as a current threat to the industry, there is the sense that events of the past continue to leave a lasting impression on the condition of South Korean cinema, its capabilities and its collective objectives. Film is used as a device to authenticate and reinforce an independent and self-determined idea of what constitutes 'the Korean' or contemporary Korean identity, and in doing so celebrates a domestic pursuit of unity—particularly with regard to an autonomous *Southern* identity (partially separate, but not entirely disconnected from, the presence of North Korea). Given South Korea's complex history and, by extension, the tumultuous journey of its cultural production, it is perhaps more necessary to recognise the benefits of 'nationalising' our readerly approach to the country's filmic pursuits in the modern age. Fundamentally, the concept of an independent nationhood, alongside an autonomous national identity, is something to be observed and preserved in all forms of South Korean popular culture (and within the landscapes it manifests).

This may act as another reason why, alongside Hollywood, it is problematic to use other East Asian cinemas as a concrete example from which to compare and contrast the cinematic creations of South Korea. While the influence of a colonial past (as a prominent historical example) is evident within many facets of national South Korean culture and consciousness, it by no means limits an increasingly comprehensive and independent notion of new Korean identity—particularly when studying film and how 'Korean-ness' is distinctively imagined on screen. The renowned ordeals of history are certainly felt and are often addressed, but not in a way that may prove detrimental or obstructive to the discovery of a positive, individualistic and cohesive national character. Instead, such narratives are often used to further investigate and solidify the concept of social wholeness.

The capital city of Seoul remains instrumental to this process, regardless of how it manifests itself or, equally, how it is manifested by others—be it as a construct, an image or a tangible space. The ever-changing and evolving city remains imperative to the formation of Korean cinematic narrative and occupies a significant space across all genres, modes and styles. As Jinhee Choi observes, 'such physical transformations of urban space and spatial disorientation are important concerns for contemporary South Korean films' and, naturally, these issues often invite contemplative discussions about cultural and national character (Choi 2016, p. 220). It is possible that the continued development and exploration of the city has helped to create new opportunities for social reflection, in which Korean identity can be viewed as a self-contained concept—partially influenced, though not entirely dictated by, past events or crises. To a large degree, Seoul embodies the modern and the contemporary. It provides a vision of the future even as it simultaneously acknowledges its own fragile past and thus cultivates a certain sense of freedom and experimentation.

If the city does, indeed, create space for the exploration of this unique Korean identity, one might surmise that it holds a utopian duality, something which cannot be as easily applied to its renowned urban neighbours: Tokyo, Beijing, etc. This duality is captured by the desire, both domestically and globally, to read Seoul as an acutely composed, constructed and artificial structure that may nonetheless be construed as an authentic, honest and distinctive South Korean landscape. In order to further unravel such a complex level of hybridity, one must begin by examining the relationship between and/or presentation of genre and the celluloid city in South Korean film and, by extension, the urban tropes contained within it.

Therefore, this book will evaluate the cinematic depiction of Seoul through five different, interpretative lenses: as a psycho-geographical space, as a generic landscape, as a hyper-masculine metropolis, as a suppressive realm (in relation to female identity) and, finally, as an oppositional space. This textual and methodological approach will create the necessary space and scope in which to conduct a nationally focused reading of post-millennial South Korean cinema. Most importantly, it will help to sustain and ultimately broaden the space in which one is able to identify the processes of localisation (be it through the emphasis of cultural signifiers or the deconstructive approach to genre discourse) that continue to define and strengthen the autonomy and power of the South Korean film industry.

References

BBC News. 2020. Oscars 2020: South Korea's Parasite Makes History by Winning Best Picture. *BBC News*. Accessed 18 February 2020. https://www.bbc.co.uk/news/entertainment-arts-51440241.

Cho, H. 2002. Sopyonje: Its Cultural and Historical Meaning. In *Im Kwon-Taek: The Making of a Korean National Cinema*, ed. David James and Kyung Hyun Kim. Detroit, MI: Wayne State University Press.

Choi, J. 2011. National Cinema: An Anachronistic Delirium? *The Journal of Korean Studies* 16 (2): 173–191. https://doi.org/10.1353/jks.2011.0012.

———. 2016. Seoul, Busan and Somewhere Near: Korean Gangster Noir and Social Immobility. In *Global Cinematic Cities: New Landscapes of Film and Media*, ed. Johan Andersson and Lawrence Webb. New York: Columbia University Press.

Gateward, F. 2007. *Seoul Searching: Culture and Identity in Contemporary Korean Cinema*. Albany: State University of New York Press.

Oh, Y. 2021. *Pop City: Korean Popular Culture and the Selling of Place*. Ithaca: Cornell University Press.

Shim, D. 2016. Hybridity and the Rise of Korean Popular Culture in Asia. *Media, Culture & Society* 28 (1): 25–44. https://doi.org/10.1177/0163443706059278.

Walsh, J. 2014. Hallyu as a Government Construct: The Korean Wave in the Context of Economic and Social Development. In *The Korean Wave: Korean Popular Culture in Global Context*, ed. Y. Kuwahara. New York: Palgrave Macmillan.

CHAPTER 2

The Psycho-geographical City

The 'city' as we know it today is a predominantly modern concept, especially so within contemporary popular culture. When the city becomes cinematic, all the significant social, cultural and historical observations contained within it are projected onto, and observed by, a diverse global audience. This two-way exchange of information means that cinema significantly contributes to, and is responsible for, our [post]modern grasp of the cityscape and, to a certain extent, the simulated image of the country that surrounds it and populace that inhabits it. As both a lived space and a cultural construction (though at times these two distinctions appear intertwined), the city exists as a functional landscape, obligated to fulfil a specific purpose, to instigate and register some kind of social and cultural development.

Concepts of the 'new', or that which exists within the 'now', are inevitably linked to this seemingly progressive urban landscape, not simply because we generally associate modern ideas with equally modern environments but because these very ideas are what essentially sustain the city itself and preclude urban immobility or stagnation. Notions of the past therefore, including the inherently romanticised narratives of nostalgia that are contained within it, are inevitability overwhelmed, though not entirely defeated, by the persistent advance of contemporary urban 'thought', which alludes to a constant, perhaps even urgent, desire for

© The Author(s), under exclusive license to Springer Nature
Switzerland AG 2023
G. Ballard, *Urban Landscapes and National Visions in Post-Millennial South Korean Cinema*, East Asian Popular Culture,
https://doi.org/10.1007/978-3-031-29739-7_2

modernisation and a universal pursuit of the new. Ironically, however, it is the critical understanding of the postmodern condition that often renders urban space as a site of undesirable social sterility and/or stasis, which ultimately posits the city as a growing repository of pre-existing textual forms, vestigial landscapes, replicable concepts and distorting ideologies. Therefore, what constitutes the 'new' in this case is as much a bi-product of cinema—a dominant, [post]modern cultural institution—as of both the city itself and our perception of it.

As Maurice Yacowar observes, 'For over a hundred years the cinema has both reflected our vision of the metropolis and helped to shape that vision—an inevitable process in a century when so much is centred on the world of city and celluloid' (Yacowar 2000, p. 273). If it has always been understood that the city exists as pure construction, as modern paradigm or indeed as 'celluloid', it is entirely possible to call into question the authenticity, inclusivity and representation of collective urban space. Filmic texts do not simply visualise, dramatise and articulate the city, but they build upon and emphasise a historically established, collective notion of urban space. Thus, to what extent a city encompasses the prevailing attitudes and beliefs of its own inhabitants, past, present and future, remains somewhat ambiguous, particularly when it is relocated, and later enhanced, on a mass-consumed cinema screen. One might question whether it is even possible for the city to exist as anything other than a postmodern construct in film as much as in reality. If we are to consider the urban landscape as a shared social construction and/or text, the term 'imagined space' (alongside the inference of imagined community) is more appropriate as it draws attention to the postmodern plight of both the city and the city resident, particularly if we are to regard 'plight' as a form of circumstance as opposed to a negative condition (Anderson 2006). After all, the foundations upon which a city is created, and later nurtured, arguably comprise a specific set of fixed cultural images, philosophies and ideological signifiers.

The more the urban landscape is addressed within popular culture, especially in cinema, the higher the probability that our own responses to such imagery will be used to further shape, create and sustain the overarching narrative of the cityscape and the many who live within it. An intense, and highly postmodern, 'reader-response' movement such as this draws attention to Barbara Mennel's argument that the cinema has an unwavering 'authority' over the 'facades and topographies of cities', which can be tracked as far back as early Twentieth-century Hollywood cinema, when the city was imagined as a dynamic backdrop, as a dominant narrative device or as a key catalyst for character movement and emotional trajectory (Mennel 2008, p. 6). The authority that Mennel refers to here is indicative of our postmodern relationship with the cinematic landscape and how the images born from this exchange might be simultaneously projected onto, and integrated within, the familiar and settled spaces of everyday life. The streets, buildings, advertisements, architecture and layout of a city are all a product of a long-established, and now universally familiar, understanding of what constitutes the 'urban environment'. This is primarily caused by a continually expanding collection of ideas that are largely informed by difference (and the deconstructive understanding that the urban encompasses, represents and delivers everything that the rural cannot). As a consequence, a self-perpetuating cycle of paradox is formed, in which one kind of cultural image is used to inform another, and vice versa. For this reason, we are again compelled to address the absolute interconnectedness between national, cultural and/or social identity and the cityscape, and more importantly, question the ways in which the latter defines the former.

It might appear culturally, socially and economically dangerous for a capital city to act as the sole representative of its own country. To judge an entire nation based upon the characteristics of such a singular and isolated space not only problematises the often heteroglossic notion of national identity (as there may be a failure to recognise the multifaceted and diverse nature of community), but it potentially diminishes the ubiquitous narrative of history. Here again, the notion of an imagined space takes social precedence. Even so, it appears as though South Korea and its capital city, Seoul, are cinematically synonymous. They remain as two landscapes that are inextricably connected, to such an extent that 'Seoul is Korea and Seoul's image is Korea's', as Colin Marshall observes (Marshall 2017). This is not surprising when considering how the social and economic growth of both the country and its capital, as well as the increasing international attention they have received, have occurred on near-parallel timelines, developing in 'tandem' (Marshall 2017).

This approach is highly relevant as it is clearly symptomatic of a shared perception of contemporary South Korea, both globally and locally. The 'tandem' development suggests that the self-cultivated image of the country has in some capacity been informed by dominant exterior influences, the conflation of once distinctive global realms and the resultant expectations of a modernising domestic society. Seoul's rate of modernisation and globalisation may be viewed as a national response to the concentrated international interest it has received in recent years, which means that, rather controversially, the urban image it has lately adopted and broadcast has been ostensibly informed by both Korean (internal) and Western (external) modes of social discourse and expectation, as the two form part of an increasingly interdependent and synergetic dialogue. This is a significant (though not entirely unexpected) development, particularly because 'Korea has been more concerned [historically] about the influx of foreign cultures—be it Japanese, Chinese or American—than the advance of its own', as Jeong Suk Joo summarises (Joo 2011, p. 489). However, one has to take into account the widening repercussions, both positive and negative, of globalisation and the ensuing level of urban competitiveness it manifests. A complex cooperative has been formed (albeit reluctantly), whereby different schools of global thought are able to interact with one another and create a distinct social conversation—an overlapping discourse between the urbanised East and West.

As a result, the state of South Korea's collective identity as a country remains ambivalent, given that the majority of national and international attention has been aimed primarily at Seoul alone. This again highlights Marshall's observation of parallel development between city and country. The cultural character and the global impression of the Korea that surrounds Seoul, whether rural or urban, has inevitably merged with the present identity of the capital, effectively creating a fusion of multifaceted and multidimensional histories and social topographies. Today, Seoul is effectively the epitomising marker against which all other Korean landscapes are measured and compared, in both cinema and general society, but this recognition has only been achieved through a process of global and domestic diplomacy.

While there have been a number of developments taking place in urban areas *outside* of Seoul (perhaps in an attempt to diversify and broaden the cultural landscape and, by extension, variegate South Korea's national identity), the capital city continues to take precedence. The cities of Busan, Incheon and Daegu, for example, have enjoyed several crucial developments over the past few years, many of which pertain to improved cultural outputs and resources. One cannot overlook the impact and importance of the Busan International Film Festival (BIFF), established in 1996, in facilitating the wider global engagement with and interest in South Korean national cinema. Even alongside these developments, however, there is a continued emphasis on Seoul as a nationally representative realm (that reflects and facilitates, to some extent, the ambitions of the government). The dominance of Seoul in Korean popular culture and politics is indicative of this. Furthermore, our knowledge of South Korea's geography as a whole is often facilitated by the continued acknowledgement of Seoul as a primary landmark/centralising compass. From a Westernised perspective, for example, any awareness of South Korea's other urban sites, such as Busan or Daegu, is largely guided, though not dictated, by continuous comparisons with the capital and its expanding population. As Yeong-Hyun Kim states, 'Seoul has long been the capital, primate city, and international gateway of Korea'; thus, it continues to be focalised within the discussions about South Korea on a broader, world basis (Kim 2004, p. 64).

There is a certain sense of Korean totality embedded within the country's principal metropolis or the feeling of a compressed and intensified national spirit located within its parameters. Unlike other capital cities, therefore, Seoul has had to negotiate, accept and, in some form, represent South Korea's historicity and vast rural landscape because, to the rest of the world at least, its own image was conceptualised *alongside* that of the country it occupies. This also demonstrates how the presentation of Seoul differs from other depictions of cinematic cities, whereby the past is respected, but not necessarily relevant or of major social and stylistic concern. Seoul by comparison has a persistent and unrelenting recognition of its own complex and occasionally traumatic past, and acknowledges the importance of preserving collective memory and keeping history firmly in place. The extent to which the city resides within a distinct place in South Korea's wider national consciousness is not to be underestimated, as the pervading narrative of the 'past' is facilitated by a dominant and united Korean cognizance, thus takes permanent and secure residence amongst an ever-expanding modern vista. Seoul's [sub]structure, or rather the deeper architectural and thus symbolic layers of the city, are illustrative of this temporal convergence, as they are built upon a set of familiar binary oppositions: old and new, tradition and modernity, the significance of the past and the promise of the future.

Seoul: The People's City

There is a two-way relationship between Seoul and those who live there—each is sustained by the other so that a fundamental interchange and communicative understanding is created. Indeed, one might argue that neither can exist in complete isolation of the other. In Kian Tajbakhsh's analysis of urban theory and identity, he observes how the city nurtures 'spaces of dwelling', and to 'dwell' in such cases is to 'live in relation to one's environment, landscape and community' (Tajbakhsh 2001, p. 7). The very term 'Seoulite' is an illustration of this postmodern notion. It demonstrates both a literal and symbolic convergence of the city and the city dweller or a timely conflation of character and actor. More importantly, however, the term 'Seoulite' places particular emphasis on the power, status and influence of the city itself, as though it lives at the heart of a centrifugal structure from which all other narratives are born and on which they are later dependent. This is demonstrative of a psycho-geographical hierarchy, in which the concept of the city precedes that of the individual and remains in a permanent fixture of higher authority. One might therefore reason that in addition to Tajbakhsh's base definition, to 'dwell' is to ultimately rely on and, to a certain extent, be governed by a greater geographical and environmental force. Thus, the city (and to an extent urban identity) undergoes a process of positive mythologisation, whereby the idea overwhelms the reality, and this transformation is afterwards inherited by its many residents. This suggests that a shared language and a harmonic existence between the city and the city dweller is not only possible, but it is integral to the preservation of identity regardless of how it manifests itself, either as an authentic creation born out of the individual or as a cultural construct reproduced and projected upon the postmodern self.

In popular culture, however, the line between the two grows increasingly blurred—particularly within South Korea's cinematic pursuits. Naturally, therefore, the exploration of the cityscape and its impact on personal and collective identity has grown to be a key constitutive element of the country's national cinematic agenda, especially so in recent years. As the global and domestic attention towards the capital has intensified, so too has the interest of the country's developing film industry, mostly likely because it has recognised the socio-cinematic potential of the city and its people. As a result of this discovery, contemporary South Korean film often posits Seoul as a purgatorial space. It presents the city as both an authentic metropolis upon which South Korea's national identity is entirely dependent, as well as a highly constructed, and cinematically functional, diegetic world in which the hyperbolic and melodramatic nature of film narrative can sufficiently unfold and thus entertain. While the consideration of the urban landscape is far from a foreign concept in most national cinemas, South Korean film seems ostensibly to take this investigation further by drawing so intensely upon the cultural, social, historical and even spiritual connections between Seoul and its diverse, inter-generational community. The city functions not only as a highly impressionistic construction *on* screen, but it also derives a perverse kind of filmic dynamism *from* it. As Cho Myung Rae observes, 'The city is a theatrical space ... where [the] grand drama of city life is performed by a mass of actors', and this theatricality is not only accepted, but it is desired (Cho 1999, p. 122). Seoul is no exception to this rule. It epitomises the concept of the cinematic city and how its filmic existence might overwhelm, and gradually eclipse, the lived and functional facets of 'true' urban space.

The inherent performativity that pervades the landscape adds yet another layer to the already complex notion of a stable identity, suggesting that it is neither authentic nor widely sought after in a strictly modern context. This raises the question of whether the artificial self is something inherited from the surrounding landscape or is a collection of cognitive responses that are willingly explored and assimilated by the individual in order to negotiate the various narratives embedded within contemporary urban existence. If the city is, indeed, a 'stage', then it might be appropriate to consider the adoption of identity, and the fluidity and changeability that this act permits, as a tool with which one might be enabled to spectacularise oneself and ultimately authenticate the inauthentic (in the postmodern mind at least). This means that the characteristics that were once considered integral to a performative identity, including those attributed to the grand postmodern narrative, gradually become normalised and, to a certain extent, desired. Here we can begin to see how both the cinematic city and the city that exists in lived 'reality' appear to share the same cultural responsibilities, and so the distinction between the two spaces grows ever more tenuous. Similarly to the city it is representing, the Seoul that exists in South Korean film remains an intensely postmodern and performative canvas: a highly mappable landscape, fraught with sharp edges, frames within frames and bountiful reflections, in which recognisable landmarks are used not only to serve specific narrative purposes but also demonstrate the postmodern ease with which 'reality', and the many identities that exist within it, might be transferred from one cultural platform to another.

Considering this, it would therefore be more useful to differentiate 'space' and 'place' when attempting to define the socio-geographical and socio-cultural characteristics of Seoul and its extensively hybridised landscape. 'Space' draws attention to a fundamental sense of construction and functionality, and this coincides with the purely cinematic and/or narrative purposes of Seoul and its diverse cultural plains. Academically speaking, the term is useful when examining Seoul from a solely Westernised perspective, as it not only inaugurates the necessary level of distance (between reader and text) required for critical analysis but also places emphasis on the purely spatial qualities of the city, thus enabling us to separate the authentic, lived and indigenous interior of an expansive South Korea from the intensely visual, abstract and hyper-real image of Seoul as an all-encompassing globalised state. 'Place', on the other hand, highlights an emotional connection between the self and the city, in which a foregrounding of familiarity and belonging is sustained within each individual city dweller. Fundamentally, 'place' has connotations of home and family, and thus remains somewhat of an enigma to an outsider. It can only truly be understood by a native of the city, particularly by someone who has witnessed its expansion from architectural, social and cultural infancy. Essentially, Seoul as a 'place' differs depending on how it is perceived by the individual—for each Seoulite there is a very specific and personal version of the city. Thus, if 'space' provides a wider, 'bird's-eye' critique of the cityscape and its inherent postmodernity, 'place' heavily counteracts this by encouraging us to return to the ground level and explore the urban subjectivism that exists on every street, in every house and through every window.

It is possible that both Seoul and its multifaceted populace encompass both of these spatial parameters and, perhaps more importantly, there is a certain sense of collective awareness of this, both inside and outside the urban community. A conflation of the personal and the collective narrative occupies each historically distinctive area of the city so that the binary structures that dictate the key signifiers of 'space' and 'place' can be identified in equal measure. This appropriately coincides with Edward Soja's 'Spatial Trialectics' and the discovery of 'Thirdspace', which addresses the notion of 'lived, perceived and conceived' realities (Soja 1996). As Soja states, 'social space' can be seen 'entirely as mental space, [or] an "encrypted reality"', which suggests that there is a growing reliance upon a formulaic, perhaps even methodological, approach to how urban space is deciphered, read and further materialised (Soja 1996, p. 63). Contemporary urbanity might be viewed as a cooperative of different thought processes, ideas and cultural imaginings. 'Thirdspace', on the other hand, which takes into account the apparent unification of both the real and the imaginary, of truth and construction, offers an intensified version of this spatial reading. Here might be the appropriate point at which we solidify the differences between Seoul and 'Seoul' and observe how, through processes of extreme globalisation and modernisation, the latter begins to take cultural and social precedence. 'Seoul's' physical and symbolic amalgamation of real and imagined zones means that it does, on every level, fulfil the criteria of thirdspace, and this also draws attention to a resounding sense of postmodernity. The city is both 'distinguishable from other spaces' and a 'transcending composite of all spaces' (Soja 1996). It comprises equal parts familiar and unfamiliar, habitual and abstract. However, this should not be understood as a negative component of the city space, nor should it be used to infer a level of national inconsistency or lack of cultural, social and generational unity. It more so demonstrates a desire and collective will to take control of South Korea's national image and narrative—a right that has been denied to many South Korean citizens throughout recent history. Seoul, be it as a constructed or 'real' space, functions as an inclusive, trans-historical realm. A place that now evolves *alongside* the people.

The primary way that Seoul differs from other cityscapes, however, is through the perceived understanding, both internally and externally (inside and outside the city, domestically and globally), that this alternative space functions as an intentional, communally conscious and resolute pursuit towards a universal and accessible urbanity. The desire to find, cultivate and nurture something that may resemble thirdspace, with all its spatial, social and imagined intricacies, demonstrates how, above all else, cities must continue to exist as sites of excitement and radical social mobility—they must fulfil the expectations that other spaces cannot. When considering its role within millennial South Korean cinema, 'Seoul' as a construction, a concept, a space or even as a word takes on a whole new level of meaning. It manifests a discourse different from any other and works to continuously enforce its own hegemonic narrative in a manner that passes as culturally faithful yet cinematically sensationalised, thus outwardly satisfying domestic and international audiences alike. Hence, a 'Seoul Genre' is effectively created, which alludes to any body of cultural work, both on and off the cinema screen, that specifically addresses the condition, concept and/or construction of the city and its people. Thus, thirdspace in this particular context equates to a highly specific urban discourse and draws attention to a critical and inimitable relationship between the cinematic Seoul and contemporary Korean identity and culture.

In Dal Yong Jin's exploration of the globalisation of modern Korean cinema, 'the third space' is also addressed, though not in a way that directly links to Edward Soja's definition (Jin 2010). Here, 'thirdspace' notably exists as one word and one concept. While Soja's usage of the term refers to a conceptual, postmodern and imagined version of the urban/city landscape, Jin's discussion expands on Homi Bhabha's investigation of 'the third space' and uses it to focus more specifically on the link between the aforementioned theory and the hybridisation of Korean cinema, both in style and as a local film industry (Bhabha 1994). This argument in particular proves to be a more direct reflection of the 'Seoul Genre'. It is clear, however, that both Soja's and Jin's perspectives on spatiality, when considered alongside one another, highlight an increased interdependence between the construction or development of Seoul (as a domestic space and/or a global concept) and the broader impact of Korean popular culture.

It is at this stage that the Korean film industry significantly diverges from its fellow national cinemas, including those long established within East Asia. These illustrations of an alternative [third] space not only draw attention to a growing Korean pursuit towards social, cultural and cinematic fluidity, they demonstrate an emphatic ownership of, and control over, national hybridity. Jin states that in the two most recent periods of Korean filmmaking—from 1995 to 2001 and 2002 onwards—there has been an exponential increase in stylistic hybridity, which has ultimately allowed the industry to 'challenge Hollywood films', 'develop local identities' and thus create 'the third space' (Jin 2010, p. 61). By at once incorporating and defamiliarising the established paradigms of Hollywood cinema, then embedding this form within a culturally distinctive narrative, the Korean film industry is able to gradually solidify its own complex and unique identity, entirely on its own terms.

The multifaceted city of Seoul works in a similar way. Jin continues by stating that hybridity, whether cultural, social or cinematic, does not only refer to a fusion of 'different elements', but it can be used as a tool to design a 'culturally faceless whole', in which 'new connections' are discovered and sustained (Jin 2010, p. 57). Of course, with 'facelessness' comes a certain element of anonymity and therefore freedom, and it is arguable that Seoul currently exists as a state of perpetual development or a blank canvas upon which a bounty of texts can integrate and flourish. The postmodern plight of the city (which refers to circumstance rather than a negative condition) does not necessarily equate to an erasure of identity, nor does it infer or concretise social sterility. By contrast, the question of what constitutes a coherent Korean identity certainly still exists, though perhaps not in the initially negative way prominent postmodern criticism would have us believe.

Collectively, this suggests that while the enigma that is South Korea's national character remains the same, the distinctive acknowledgement of such, both globally and locally, warrants a different kind of investigative approach. Even though the notion of 'thirdspace' might further complicate one's understanding of Korea's collective identity, and possibly trouble the modern Seoulite's independent view of the self, it is still entirely possible to locate truth and authenticity within these spaces of postmodernity and performativity—and this seems to be a recurring theme in many millennial Korean films. Thus, 'Seoul' as a genre, lifestyle, narrative or perceived reality is not necessarily a contribution to South Korea's postmodern condition, it is instead a device with which we might measure the nation's response towards, and exploration of, its own complex psycho-geographical state.

Diegetic and Non-diegetic Identities: Rethinking the Relationship Between Audience and Character

Kim Ki-Duk's 2004 film *3-Iron* serves as a timely response to South Korea's concerns and questions about identity (or the diminishment of a *perceived* identity), as well as its often fluctuating position within Seoul. Marketed as a romance drama with clear art-house parallels, the film provides an anthropomorphic presentation of Seoul, in the sense that it appears to inherit certain animal-like, perverse and, above all else, living qualities. The city presented to us has feelings and emotions—it is beyond the control of the characters, the narrative and even the spectator. It demonstrates the extent to which the active (and alive) urban landscape shapes modern Korean identity or the collective perception of it. Certainly, *3-Iron* qualifies as a significant contribution to the 'Seoul Genre', as its distinctive characterisation of the city is often narratively, symbolically and stylistically foregrounded. The two characters that the story follows, whilst focalised to a certain extent, are not as central to the narrative as their complex environment. They remain functional beings, important in the sense that, like the spectator, they too must learn to negotiate the grand urban narrative, or more specifically the grand 'postmodern' narrative, that the film endeavours to portray and dramatise.

During one particular sequence, the two main characters, Tae Suk and Sun Hwa, enter the house of a deceased elderly gentleman. Upon seeing his lifeless body, they quickly compose themselves before deciding to embalm him in a faux-familial yet highly traditional act of grievance, during which there is a momentary period of reflection occurring on both sides of the filmic space. The spectator's experience here parallels that of the two characters; thus, the nature of the event is transferred from one boundary to another and, as a result, the emotion it inspires is far from a one-sided occurrence. There is an emphatic sense of emptiness that pervades the space on screen (physical, spiritual and emotional). The walls of the residence are bare, the doors made of a dark, aged wood and the little light that fills the space is provided only by a small window. Like the characters, even the eye of the camera itself appears dwarfed by the seeming vacuity and minimalism of the room. Unlike the bustling urban exterior that surrounds the residence, this isolated and highly claustrophobic space appears entirely unaffected by modern existence. There is a curious stillness to the diegesis, and more importantly, a sense that history (which largely includes Korea's historical identity) is momentarily obstructing the progress of the present story-world. The narrative that the audience has engaged with up until this point is quickly suspended as they commit to sharing the experience with the characters, who appear quietly shocked and openly solemn at having come into symbolic contact with the past—a point in time that has so greatly influenced their present state, whether they realise it or not.

There is a conflation of two very different sets of identities occurring in this moment—a meeting point of two different worlds, two diverged stories and two alternate states of Korean selfhood. The strangely purgatorial couple represents one component of this pivotal meeting. They symbolise a modern Korea, drifting from place to place, transforming alongside the ever-changing landscape, never quite settling on one final destination, and perhaps never having the wish to do so. Whether their ability to temporarily occupy these diverse spaces demonstrates a freedom of exploration or an insubstantial transience is something that remains unclear. It appears that, initially, the film does paint each character as a lost soul, searching for something that is neither tangible nor within reach. After all, while Tae Suk and Sun Hwa are enabled briefly to adopt the identities of, and live vicariously through, the tenants of the homes in which they venture, there is a constant sense that they are static, that they do not belong or have no enduring position within society.

Meanwhile, the deceased man, whose polarised position counteracts the couple in every way, signifies a constant and unchanging cultural identity, a fragment of South Korea that, though perhaps undermined by an accelerating modernity, has never entirely ceased to exist in the current urban landscape. The way in which the film imparts a strong sense of national constancy and fidelity using this character creates an immediate and universal feeling of relief. While it might be argued that *3-Iron* endeavours to approach the question of Korean identity from a fairly impartial position, this particular scene evokes a critical sense of historical recognition and a decisive aura of nationalism. Like the characters, we are heartened to find that, in any capacity, this particular being or identity has somehow survived the demands and challenges of a constantly changing landscape. His loss, therefore, feels all the more poignant.

The scene is laden with symbolic and stylistic gravity, not least because the dialogue, which up until this point has been minimal, becomes practically non-existent. Any kind of communicative device or narrative exposition is no longer required, as the event is designed to evoke a certain response from the audience. To deliver such a scene with conventional and generic techniques of cinematic story-telling would inevitably result in a process of mitigation, diminishing both the overarching message and the audience's reaction to it. Minimalism is not simply used for dramatic effect, but it is necessary in order to foreground the symbolic weight of the character—all that exists within the diegesis is effectively compromised because of his death. This is accentuated by the sense of a peculiar temporal shifting. Everything seems slightly out of place, as though Tae Suk, Sun Hwa and the audience have stepped back in time or have quite literally opened a time capsule. The temporal environment that we are exposed to in this particular moment differs greatly from the rest of the film. Here, time is dramatically *divorced* from space, narrative and character, leaving Tae Suk and Sun Hwa in an isolated, albeit purifying, sphere of existential limbo. Evidently, it seems that the characters are not simply shedding tears for the death of a stranger, but they are mourning the loss of something much greater—the loss of a South Korea that 'used to be'.

The death of the man and the circumstances in which he is found, alone and distanced from a family that no longer cares, signify a forgotten Korea or the gradual diminishment of a specific kind of Korean identity, one that is intrinsically linked to the nostalgic past. Nevertheless, this is arguably the point at which the film's inherent nostalgia and romanticism overshadow the dominant concerns of South Korea's history and its historical identity, both of which are unquestionably represented by the elderly character. Moments that appear sombre and demand reflection are often diffused by a conventional sentimentality not dissimilar to the 'conscience liberalism' displayed by standard Hollywood fare, whereby impartiality transforms into blissful ignorance (Maltby 2003). Although it is clear the function of the scene is to evoke a certain kind of sadness within the spectator, this emotion is never fully validated by any narrative cause or exposition. While this may be attributed to the tendencies of abstract modernist cinema, the purpose of the sequence (to measure the validity of one kind of Korean identity against another) requires a certain amount of stylistic lucidity (which refers to a need for narrative exposition). However, this is not to be. We do not know, for example, where the elderly man is from, who his family is or what happened in the final stages of his life, yet it is still clear that the death of the character is significant—and the film wants us to recognise this. The loss of 'another Korea' is apparent and highly lamentable; exactly what kind of 'Korea' this may be, significantly less so.

The notion of identity (and national identity) becomes a familiarised, perhaps even generic, narrative trope and exists as a collection of mythologising ideas. The question of what constitutes authentic identity is perhaps no longer of primary concern. Instead, *3-Iron* uses this pivotal scene to address the *relevance* of identity itself and explore the various ways it can function in the modern world, especially in modern South Korea. The desire to 'look back' and establish one's own history, place and narrative seems to be a continuing thread not only in Korean film but within many national cinemas. However, this particular sequence is accompanied by a general sense of sadness, as though loss is both inevitable and irreversible. There is clearly an emphatic yearning for clarity happening in this moment, a need to understand what 'Korean-ness' actually is and, more importantly, how it might sustain itself within the increasingly modernising parameters of millennial Seoul and alongside its many inhabitants.

In this respect, *3-Iron* is certainly a story of two halves. Its celebration of South Korea's intensely hybridised contemporary landscape is matched only by its equal longing to preserve the past and uphold the importance of the country's complex history. The death scene, therefore, though in many ways tragic (due to the suggestion that the character has been subjected to an unprecedented level of loneliness), functions as a catalyst for a cathartic act of remembrance. Thus, identity is no longer a question of simply adopting character or mobilising a certain ideology. Nor is it ascertaining a specific belief system that fits into the contemporary social climate. It is instead an exploration of how the past can be unearthed in the present and how memory might be allowed to continually exist within Korea's [post]modern social consciousness and expanding urbanity. Only by seeking out and further stabilising the past can the identities of a nation, of a city and, indeed, of the individual learn to negotiate the intensifying, though not necessarily threatening, force of postmodernity.

REINSTATING THE SELF: *3-IRON*'S CHALLENGE TO COLLECTIVE POSTMODERN THOUGHT

Although it is arguable that the postmodern condition posits a certain erasure or homogenisation of identity, the order of events in *3-Iron* suggests that it is possible to sustain one's own personal narrative, individuality and authentic 'self', even amidst an increasingly hyper-real landscape. This distorts the commonly sterile and cynical view of contemporary urban existence inaugurated by postmodern criticism. By contrast, the film demonstrates how identity (or the absence of it) is something which cannot necessarily be fixed or predetermined by outsider imagery alone. Cho Myung Rae identifies Seoul and 'the body of the Seoulite' as having a 'schizophrenic identity', in which different social codes and values exist together, though not necessarily in a consistent or harmonious way (Cho 1999, p. 130). This results in a fractured portrait of the self, where various personalities, attitudes or beliefs inevitably clash and collide. While it is certainly appropriate to consider Seoul as a single space, site or 'body' of immense social heteroglossia, especially when considering the city from a purely psycho-geographical perspective, the use of the word 'schizophrenic' as a primary descriptive marker here indicates an altogether more irrational and fragile state of Korean identity. Even though Cho's argument illustrates and emphasises the 'multifaceted' nature of the self, the existing connotations of the term 'schizophrenia' cast an anxious, perhaps even condemnatory, gaze over the present structure of Seoul's comprehensive identity. It denotes a lack of control and awareness, as though the identity of the city and its vast populace is something inherently vulnerable, unpredictable and conflicted. A stigmatised, even ostracised, view of identity is thus introduced and exists as a repressed undercurrent of social consciousness. Contrary to this, *3-Iron* continuously attempts to unveil the various schisms hidden within the modern Korean psyche which, while initially appearing detrimental to a coherent, stable and characteristically distinctive identity, remain a facet of the self that is to be embraced rather than oppressed.

There are, for example, continual allusions to the 'self', and to the image of the 'self', dispersed throughout the entirety of *3-Iron*. Tae Suk's first encounter with the abused housewife Sun Hwa is established only by her photograph. Even from this early stage, it is her image that has taken precedence over her real form in Tae Suk's mind and also, perhaps more interestingly, from the audience's perspective too. This is indicative of a postmodern layering of textual identity. Our only knowledge of Sun Hwa's character at this point is delivered to us via three separate visual veils: the photograph, Tae Suk's response to it and finally, the manner in which this relationship is communicated and transported from the filmic world to the non-diegetic space in which we are positioned. Thus, the way identity is established here is primarily through transposition; every narrative detail is passed on through an acutely composed journey of visual cues, each filtered by a different image. This is also emphasised by the abundance of reflections and apparent symmetry that appear in the film, whether in the windows of Seoul's many high-rise buildings, the glass frames that adorn the walls of a photographer's minimalist apartment or the side-view mirrors on Tae Suk's motorcycle (which seem to offer a fantastical insight into a parallel world, where nothing is ever stationary).

Jean-Jacques Beineix's *Diva* (1981) engages with urban surfaces in a similar way. Both this text and *3-Iron* present the cityscape as having a stage-like quality, in which there are constant allusions to the reproduction and replication of imagery and a general sense of artifice. In *Diva*, however, Paris is a replicable blank parody at the centre of the postmodern gaze and is perhaps not treated in the same self-referential and occasionally cynical manner that Seoul is in *3-Iron*. The various exteriors and faces of the latter act as constant reminders that everything we see remains perpetually obstructed by another surface or object. Ultimately, this means our perspective of the diegetic world, as well as the impression of the characters that exist within it, is forever invaded by another image and/or narrative.

Therefore, reality, narrative and language are ultimately infinite. They are never articulated in their entirety. Indeed, Kim Soh-Youn argues that 'what is remarkable [in the film] is the strategy of its imaging screen employing mirroring materials ... to illustrate how subjectivity is alienated and later liberated' (Kim 2014, p. 106). Just because we as the viewer, alongside Tae Suk and Sun Hwa, experience *3-Iron's* enigmatic Seoul through an isolated and transient kind of motion, it does not mean that our subjective response is any less valid, nor is the shared identity that the two characters finally discover for themselves any less genuine or plausible. The manner in which the film establishes, presents and meanders through the urban landscape is a direct reference to the physical construction of any city environment, as well as a true reflection of the city dweller's daily postmodern interaction with it. Glass surfaces, windows, technological advertisements, photographs and countless cultural imagery offer only a temporary glimpse of what lies on the other side, behind the physical and symbolic surface. Thus, knowledge in the urban environment is only half acquired because each signifier that is presented before the spectator offers only a partial insight. It is essentially up to the individual viewer to decide whether to commit and venture further in order to attain the finished narrative. *3-Iron's* engagement with, and representation of, Seoul's urbanity and complex identity works very much in the same way. Each home that Tae Suk and Sun Hwa enter comprises a specific set of visual signifiers that, collectively, allow us to create a narrative or imagine a particular scenario befitting of the film's general tone, style or aesthetic. The subject in question, however, which in this case would be the home-owner, remains almost entirely absent. Thus, the enigma is, to some extent, sustained.

There is a postmodern duality that exists as an omniscient presence on both sides of the diegesis. While the characters learn to negotiate their own postmodern conditions *inside* of the filmic space, we as an audience are exposed to the postmodern style and delivery that remains extremely prevalent *outside* of it. More importantly, this self-awareness is not something that is necessarily specific to *3-Iron*. While one might attribute the film's minimalistic and reflective aesthetic to Kim Ki-Duk's art-house tendencies as a director, and to the paradigmatic characteristics of art film universally, it seems as though these decisions form part of a larger and expanding allegorical trend within South Korea's national cinematic identity. This also demonstrates how Korean cinema is able to localise global film discourses and ultimately, defamiliarise the familiar. While Tae Suk and Sun Hwa may initially appear to embody certain generic roles that might be considered archetypal of any melodrama (the enigmatic loner and the isolated housewife), they function as transgressive beings and therefore complicate the paradigms and tropes of standard characterisation—namely those associated with the principles of more traditional Hollywood practice.

The film remains very much aware of this and instead utilises each character to address, in a highly self-reflexive manner, the absolute interconnectedness of postmodernity, performativity and identity in both film and 'real' life. This suggests that even though one might adhere to the certain criteria of a social role or fulfil the requirements of an established social performance (which common postmodern criticism suggests we all do), identity can still remain determined and, to a certain extent, controlled by the individual. Most importantly, however, *3-Iron* presents urban identity as a 'concept' and with it, the city as a space in which the ideas that surround us and/or them might unfold and collide. This, in turn, further solidifies the notion of urban landscape as predominantly imagined space. Thus, Seoul becomes increasingly hybridised—a place where different identities (or bodies of ideas and abstractions) are drawn to, and stimulated by, fixed areas of the cityscape. These existential ideas are evidenced in the film by the various homes and public spaces that are explored, all of which serve a different cultural, social and, in some cases, historical function.

While this observation exemplifies the earlier discussion on Tajbakhsh's 'spaces of dwelling' in the city, Tae Suk and Sun Hwa are characters that significantly complicate this structural approach to the understanding of the relationship between the city and the individual. Tajbakhsh's argument, whilst highly appropriate when considering how the urban environment creates and nurtures postmodern identities, relies upon a fundamental sense of familiarity or social fluency (Tajbakhsh 2001, p. 7). To 'dwell' in the city is to ultimately have a habitual, even ritualistic, relationship with one's own environment—to forge a spatial and temporal harmony with a specific urban site. This may not be so difficult to achieve if we are to believe that the city itself, or at least the cultural conception of it, is an image designed by our own epistemological understanding of urban space and/or existence. The inherent paradox of this relationship ultimately means that no matter how much the cityscape may change, progress or alter, which it undoubtedly does, the typical urban resident grows to expect this and undergoes a constant process of transformation and adaptation. This continues to the point where even the continual act of postmodern engagement (via social and cultural assimilation) becomes normalised or, indeed, ordinary.

Therefore, dwelling not only involves living 'in relation to' one's environment, but it also allows the environment in question to dictate the very nature of the self and, ultimately, maintain some form of subjective equilibrium. Tae Suk and Sun Hwa, on the other hand, have no such stability. This is not necessarily because they cannot manifest a functional or consistent relationship with the prevailing urban landscape, but it is because they simply have no wish to do so. To a certain extent, the characters seem to provide a touristic gaze of the city and its people: temporarily enjoyable, yet not enough to warrant prolonged exploration or to seek a sustained co-existence. Tae Suk and Sun Hwa drift from area to area, never staying in one single space long enough to truly 'dwell'. Any notion of the self, in this instance, is almost entirely determined by the purgatorial environment that they alone have endeavoured to create. This is not to say, however, that a purgatorial relationship with one's surroundings creates a negative existence, nor does it invalidate one's identity.

Frames Within Frames: The Photographic Narrative

When both characters intrude upon the residence of a professional photographer, perhaps the most meta-cinematic moment in the film, the highly intertextual and self-reflexive nature of the narrative is fully foregrounded. The small space is replete with portraits, memories and, most importantly, identities. Every corner, every wall and every surface is obtruded upon by a face, a body or an expression. Clearly, the space acts as yet another pivotal moment of reflection for Tae Suk and Sun Hwa, who at one point decide to take pictures of themselves standing next to the photographs, while we as an audience observe through the modern screen of a handheld camera. A visual layering of personae and narratives occupy the entirety of the frame, as well as an intense layering of identities, many of which belong to, and have been realised by, the secondary and subjective vision of another artistic presence—the photographer. The manner in which the apartment is presented somewhat diminishes the spectator's pre-conceived awareness of, and separation from, the diegesis, as the contrasting surfaces that occupy the space create an unprecedented level of depth and dimensionality, effectively challenging the physical and symbolic parameters of the cinema screen itself. There are narratives built *within* narratives—each photo corresponds to a specific time period, place and story. It is perhaps natural, therefore, that the two characters find solace and comfort in the space. Given that they have not yet discovered their own societal self, they can relish the opportunity to observe the many faces of those who seemingly have. The apartment acts as a fusion of creation, construction and artifice. It is filled with still or 'fixed' images and acts as a zone of duplication, or a space of apparent nothingness, upon which the characters can project and thus decipher their own states. The apartment is static and stationary, halted by the conclusive yet harmonic narratives that are contained within it.

It is suggested that this particular space is entirely and intentionally separate not only from the cinematic image of 'Seoul' that *3-Iron* endeavours to present (alongside the construct that we, the reader, produce) but also from our pre-conceived understanding of the capital as a 'real' and lived space. The small apartment represents a spatial and temporal anomaly for both the characters who are actively exploring it and the spectator who observes it. A collapsing of binaries takes place, and what essentially remains is a blank canvas—a momentary suspension of the present film narrative. While this may act as another indication of 'thirdspace', it seems that the apartment represents a significant diversion from this formulaic reading of urban spatiality. If the events prior to this moment have led us to identify a conflation between Seoul and its cinematic counterpart, thus inferring 'thirdspace', the residence exhibited in this particular scene attempts to distort this relationship or, indeed, abandon it altogether. As discussed earlier, while the notion of 'thirdspace' exists outside of the imagined city and the real/social/historical city, it is still realised and sustained via an inextricable, yet indirect, connection to and awareness of both. Here, however, the apartment in question symbolises no such dependency. The isolation and temporal peculiarities that exist within are clearly juxtaposed by the movement that exists elsewhere in the surrounding city, as well as the many identities (whether artificial, performative or authentic) that operate there.

Nevertheless, the room is not entirely foreign, nor is it a coincidental choice of temporary residence for the characters. It is only when a familiar portrait of Sun Hwa appears does the film make it clear that the photographer in question has worked with the character before this moment, presumably at the request of her volatile husband. In this scene, *3-Iron* allows the spectator to form a full and connected narrative circle, as we are reminded that the same photograph also exists in Sun Hwa's home and was initially the only means of introducing her oppressed character to both the audience and Tae Suk. No matter how seemingly arbitrary their endeavours and decisions, neither protagonist can completely escape the urban 'self' that exists as an underlying presence throughout the city. These particular identities, forged through time, are embedded within the very fabric of the metropolis. Similar to the structure of the film, Sun Hwa exists as part of a continuous and everlasting cycle/narrative and must eventually come face to face with her own (former) self. Her travels with Tae Suk, across an increasingly paradoxical urban landscape, have ultimately led to this inevitable moment. Whether this is used to infer a notion of postmodern inescapability is perhaps unclear, though it does ascertain an inextricable and inescapable link between the constructed image and the perception of identity.

In an extremely prolonged shot, she faces her own image in a mirror-like composition of perfect stillness, though it is clear she has no connection with the person or identity presented in the frame. One might consider the scene as an uncanny, self-referential and perverse allusion to Jacques Lacan's 'mirror-stage' theory, which addresses the formation of identity during infancy (Lacan 2004). Though Sun Hwa clearly does not fit this specific criterion, her isolation, lost sense of self and initial willingness to be led by another figure (i.e. Tae Suk), suggests that her character is designed to occupy a certain state of emptiness and infantilism. While this decision may purely coincide with planned narrative trajectory, it more importantly addresses a potential crisis in contemporary urban identity (and perhaps female urban identity more specifically). Not only is Sun Hwa unable to identify herself in the portrait, there is the increasing sense that she has no desire to recognise this supposed version of herself—a clear manifestation of social and cultural expectation. Even though this contemplative gaze upon the photograph may function as a reminder of the character's purgatorial and vulnerable identity, it also helps her to affirm and finalise everything that she is *not*, and thus initiates some form of positive self-recognition by default.

The short period of revelation and self-discovery created here is further emphasised by Sun Hwa's purposeful reconstruction of the portrait, whereby she cuts the photograph into squares before rearranging each piece to form an abstract collage. Tae Suk, meanwhile, looks on in wonder, appreciation and silent understanding. Upon returning the frame to its original place on the wall, it is clear that Sun Hwa's impression and vision of her own self is vastly different to that of the photographer and, presumably, her own husband. What was once a highly romanticised, coherent and manipulated human portrait is now a fragmented collection of different body parts, textures and angles. Each section appears entirely at odds with its neighbour—hand is next to eye, leg next to shoulder, black background interspersed with white skin. Yet, even amongst this barrage of surrealist redesign and artistic modernisation, Sun Hwa is still clearly identifiable and, more importantly, she appears satisfied with this self-determined and self-controlled construction of her own image. Although the picture is disordered and inconsistent, each piece of the puzzle is exactly the same size, thus demonstrating how each facet of the identity is of equal importance and no longer a site of imposed socio-cultural homogeneity.

As Kim So-Youn observes, Sun Hwa's act of defiance in this moment is used to 'express her rejection of the mastery of narrative' (Kim 2014, p. 116) and therefore draws attention to *3-Iron's* ability to significantly disrupt critical consensus by distorting the common notion that postmodernity is an all-encompassing and unmanageable 'grand-urban' condition. While such narratives are apparent and powerful, they do not necessarily dictate the structure of identity in its entirety, and it appears as though Sun Hwa realises this fact when she acknowledges her own inherent spectrality via the 'new' self-portrait. More importantly, however, one must recognise that despite the character's creative intervention, the photograph remains as a complete and absolute piece, which suggests that unity can be born from radical fragmentation. Even though each section of the collage is different and jarring, when placed alongside each other, they form an undivided and harmonic whole. There is a sense that the character is 'reborn' in this moment and is no longer a mere vacuous archetype designed to support the leading male protagonist. An equilibrium is established between Tae Suk and Sun Hwa, and this connection grows more intense as the film nears its end.

Indeed, by *3-Iron's* conclusion, any notion of language, narrative or text is rendered completely redundant and is instead replaced by a sense of sublime spirituality or otherworldliness. After the couple are eventually caught and arrested for trespassing, Sun Hwa returns home with her husband (though, of course, as a completely different being). Tae Suk, meanwhile, after a long period of time, appears to acquire what can only be described as a magical ability to evade the naked eye and is therefore able to escape prison. At this stage, the film goes beyond stylistic postmodernism, perhaps even beyond the territories of art cinema, and turns into something entirely more difficult to define. When Tae Suk returns to Sun Hwa, it is only as a ghostly presence who she alone can see and interact with. This means that alongside the seeming 'reality' that is occupied by the outside world, including Sun Hwa's oblivious husband, the two protagonists have ultimately established their own disconnected realm. They have created another platform of communication, a different world that inhabits a separate layer of the diegesis. Even though this may compromise the lived and 'authentic' spaces previously established in the film, it more importantly demonstrates how the two characters have inherited the positive traits of the cityscape and projected them onto a much smaller and more intimate space.

Sun Hwa's once oppressive household is now a site of intensely layered realities and identities (or, perhaps, 'non-identities' and 'non-binaries'). While her seemingly submissive position in relation to her husband is still evident, she now realises that this aspect of her 'self' is simply performative and is used as a tool with which to satisfy a narrative that, though difficult to escape from completely, no longer dictates the fundamentals of her own identity. One might even argue that the film takes a subtle Marxist turn here, as it shows two beings that are hyper-aware of a prevailing ideological system and are therefore more inclined to ascertain their own separation from it. As Bert Cardullo observes, this positive estrangement from society has only been achieved through the 'mystical bond' forged between the two characters—a 'bond that itself contrasts with the worldliness of the city through which it winds' (Cardullo 2007). However, one might also surmise that in escaping one kind of ideology or predetermined 'space', the characters succeed only in erecting, encountering or entering another.

Regardless of the existential position the film takes by this conclusion, what remains of utmost importance is the new diegetic space that is controlled solely by the two beings who 'dwell' within it. Unbeknownst to the husband, Tae Suk meanders through the house, living unconventionally, though entirely harmoniously, alongside Sun Hwa. They conduct their own domesticated lives, though in an entirely postmodern and countersocial way. Marital bliss is certainly evident, but it is manifested and sustained in a way that simultaneously adheres to and distorts the recognisable behaviours of such a relationship, particularly because Sun Hwa's husband still occupies the household, as a vacuous third being. In the final shot, Sun Hwa gazes slightly over and behind her abusive partner's shoulder, who then mistakenly thinks that his wife's utterance of 'I love you', and following embrace, are meant for him. The profession is actually aimed at Tae Suk, who stands silently behind him. This final exchange, combined with the manner in which is it captured by the camera, acts as a visual culmination of the existential ideas addressed throughout the film. The two characters, who at this point seem to share one spiritual identity, face each other in perfect symmetry, separated only by a presence that now occupies an entirely different spatial and temporal sphere. It seems as though there are two parallel realities inhabiting the house, running alongside each other, equally powerful, yet never coming into contact.

The first existential 'plane' is recognised via the diegesis itself, which is established as soon as the film begins and concerns the familiar filmic world in which the narrative unfolds. The second 'plane', however, is introduced only in the conclusion and inhabited by Tae Suk and Sun Hwa alone. More importantly, it is also visible to the audience, which suggests that there is a duality unfolding within the diegesis at this point. Again, the film is drawing attention to texts *within* texts here, which suggests that the notion of a hybridised identity is not a singularly human concern (which refers to individual experience or personal consciousness), but it can also be seen within the physical spaces we venture into, no matter how temporary the visit. Ultimately, this coincides with Tae Suk and Sun Hwa, who appear to have adopted some of the characteristics of a transformative cityscape, in which there is constant fluidity between narrative, identity and social expectation. Had their time together taken place in rural South Korea, in a quiet village or isolated town, the conclusive 'state' of the characters would vastly differ and their revelations of the 'self' remain practically non-existent. This is because *3-Iron* draws so intensely upon the notion that modern [Korean] identity is largely moulded by the awareness and integration of an increasing urbanity in everyday life. Tae Suk and Sun Hwa are not changed due to their relationship with each other, not even with their former selves; they are changed because of Seoul and its extremely active, alive and characterful disposition—a force that has quite literally penetrated the entire ethos of both beings.

The narrative equilibrium that is established by the end of the film attempts to reinforce and essentially concretise this idea of positive urban assimilation. Though it may not be the ending that one would expect, especially when considering how the sudden 'fantasy' element is introduced, one can clearly identify a correlation between the final trajectory of the characters and the complex environment they have been exposed to prior to their reunion. Tae Suk's 'otherworldly' attributes act as a magnified and hyperbolic representation of the spirituality evident in *3-Iron's* unique depiction of Seoul. His invisible entry into the home, via a kind of spiritual osmosis, also represents an extension of the couple's previous ventures into, and appreciation of, private domestic space. Fundamentally, the city now exists *within* Tae Suk—a symbolic inheritance of landscape, culture and ethereal consciousness. We are again reminded of certain events within the film, such as the encounter with the deceased elderly man, when the supposed 'reality' of the diegesis is made somewhat vulnerable, and there is a persistent sense that a greater existential idea is imposing upon the present narrative. Upon reflection, therefore, the 'magical' aspect of the conclusion, whilst momentarily jarring and unexpected, demonstrates a cathartic culmination and realisation of the philosophies addressed throughout the film, specifically those attributed to the cinematic city and Seoul.

On a more textual level, however, the ending also shows yet another level of generic distortion, as, while a 'happy ending' is evident, it is by no means delivered in a conventional way. There are certain idiosyncrasies riddled throughout *3-Iron*, often born from the characters and their responses to particular events and, of course, to the cityscape itself. Thus, we become concerned not only with the questions raised within the narrative but also the alternative manner in which they are addressed. Tae Suk's conclusive 'state' is indicative of this. While some questions are inevitably left unanswered, others are resolved in a highly self-aware and irrational style, and this is arguably the point at which *3-Iron*, similarly to the city it endeavours to explore, sustains its own level of symbolic ambiguity, via its ability to defamiliarise the familiar.

3-Iron's Important Role in Our Broader Understanding of South Korean Cinema and Its Engagement with Seoul/the Cityscape

When attempting to establish its own distinguishable identity, South Korean cinema arguably faces more obstacles than most. Not only does it have to differentiate itself from the ever dominant Hollywood model (as, indeed, all national cinemas inevitably have to do), it must then fight to separate itself, to a stylistic extent, from its geographical neighbours while simultaneously striving to have its directors and producers recognised alongside a now long-established and highly revered East Asian cinematic canon. Park Chan Wook (*Oldboy*, *Stoker*, *The Handmaiden*) and Bong Joon Ho (*The Host*, *Snowpiercer*, *Okja*) are perhaps the only modern filmmakers who have achieved this on both a global and domestic scale in recent years, though their films are still measured by their ability to fit into a specifically 'East Asian' aesthetic, which itself is something largely developed by heavily Westernised perspectives and readings. While these interpretations do, of course, sustain their own justifiable academic gravity, they still approach the East Asian model with a fundamental level of 'othering', even though it is clear that, now more than ever, East Asian cinema has a key role in dictating the movement of commercial film discourse on both sides of the Pacific. As Chi-Yun Shin and Julian Stringer observe, from its very beginnings, the Korean film industry has had to contend with the 'ubiquitous presence of Hollywood within its marketplace' and this has resulted in the indigenisation and localisation of popular and/or generic film models (Shin and Stringer 2007, p. 55). One has to therefore question exactly to what extent these globally recognised Korean texts actually represent the country in which they have been made, given that there has always been this conversation between, and acknowledgement of, different national cinemas and their many characteristics. It is perhaps common knowledge that Kim Ki-Duk's catalogue of films, whilst achieving a degree of success internationally, have never been quite so well received domestically, and this unfavourable outlook has inevitably been magnified within the last few years due to the wave of controversies surrounding the director.[1]

From an 'outside' perspective, his films may appear Korean or seem to capture a specific kind of Korean identity (and this level of generalisation, whilst problematic, is not necessarily a negative). From 'within', however, the acknowledgement of his films as key national texts is often highly contested. As Chung Hye Seung summarises, 'Kim Ki-Duk's international fame did little to improve the box-office performance of his independently produced art films in his homeland', and since his unsuccessful debut, 'the majority of the [Korean] public has either ignored or denounced his films' (Chung 2010, p. 99). In this particular case, context has overwhelmed text, and for many reasons, rightly and justifiably so. *3-Iron,* nevertheless, whether viewed positively or negatively, remains a pivotal and important film. It deserves to be read as a text independent not only from the infamous director with whom it is associated but also from his broad

---

[1] This is in reference to several historic allegations of misconduct made against Kim Ki-Duk, which include bullying, coercion, poor work ethics and sexual harassment. While it is always important to recognise and condemn such abuses of power, for the purposes of this particular book (and in relation to the readings of *3-Iron*), one must still acknowledge Kim's films as vital components of the South Korean film industry's development in the post-millennial age and his role within the 'new wave' movement.

catalogue of other, significantly less palatable, work. Indeed, one may use the film as a strong counteraction to our understanding of auteur theory, given that it demands a certain kind of diversified analysis—a distinctive exchange between text and spectator which ultimately renders the 'author' as a fairly redundant figure.

Kim Ki-Duk certainly 'created' *3-Iron* and its characters, but by no means does this infer complete ownership. While the narrative, style and appearance of *3-Iron* have clearly been controlled by the decisions of a distinctive filmmaker, the highly personal responses to (and readings of) the text need not be subjected to the same kind of singular influence. Even though the experimental style, tone and narrative arc of the film are made fairly obvious from the opening stages, the spectator for whom these cinematic characteristics are intended is arguably less apparent. It is difficult to assign a specific kind of audience to *3-Iron*, perhaps more so a distinctive *Korean* audience (which may, in some capacity, be attributed to the text's subversive treatment of genre and thus, lack of mass marketability). The absence of an established viewership, however, is arguably what allows the film to exist far beyond the reputation of its director. As it does not meet the pre-conceived expectations of any single audience, *3-Iron* can be read in a bounty of different ways, on both a global and local scale. Therefore, the authority and artistic vision of Kim Ki-Duk, whilst evident, is somewhat diminished by each individual reaction to the narrative, and more importantly, to the array of different identities that are introduced within it.

The film never attempts to establish 'Korean-ness' as a single or finite concept. In fact, by establishing Seoul as a primary visual metaphor, *3-Iron* presents and celebrates Korean identity as an infinitely complex and extraordinary fusion of different attitudes, ideas and histories (something that *Parasite* [2019] also does, albeit in a manner that is far less fluid). *3-Iron* is consistent in its acknowledgement of its own inconsistencies, which is not to say that the modern Korean self lacks a certain sense of distinctiveness or wholeness, only that it recognises and sustains its own temporal and symbolic hybridity. Just as each space of the city is equally important and valid, so too is each facet of the country's multifaceted yet cohesive identity, regardless of whether it is born from the past, present or future. In light of this, one might argue that despite the reservations and controversies, the film should be of cultural and social interest because it is so determined to draw attention to the inclusive nature of Korea's national consciousness. At the heart of its narrative, *3-Iron* also acknowledges the absolute and unwavering influence of Seoul and the urban landscape. Though it presents the cinematic city as an uncanny and otherworldly space, its narrative remains at 'ground-level' and focuses on the individual stories embedded deeply within the maze-like metropolis. At no point is the spectator forced into a position of distance or omniscience, we remain aligned with the characters and their journey of exploration throughout. Therefore, while its style and form might be considered unconventional (in the sense that dialogue is absent and filmic enigmas are prevalent), the fairly wholesome message that is communicated by the conclusion is not. Resolution and equilibrium are established on both sides of the diegesis in the final moments, though in a manner that upholds the defamiliarising qualities introduced from the beginning. Here we can again identify the textual postmodernity that is interspersed throughout the film and, more importantly, the way it simultaneously respects and repels thematic, symbolic and stylistic expectation, resulting in something new and, it seems, distinctively *Korean* (hence the aforementioned 'Seoul Genre').

Though it should by no means be considered a singularly influential text, *3-Iron* does contribute towards a larger body of Korean work that has significantly shaped the way in which the cinematic city is both constructed and read—on an international and domestic level. The recognition that the film and its director have received, whether highly critical or complimentary, is indicative of this. There seems to be a renewed interest in the treatment of urban landscapes within Korean film, and how such environments can be used to transform the familiar paradigms of narrative, character and, most importantly, genre. *3-Iron*, alongside many other contemporary Korean films, recognises the problematic nature of film categorisation and the desire to identify certain generic concepts. The city and Seoul, therefore, are used as a self-reflexive device to complicate these structures and approaches. This includes the primary characteristics of art cinema (the genre with which *3-Iron* is perhaps most commonly associated).

Nevertheless, the film remains very much aware of this and as a result, appears to invest in a level of thematic and textual oscillation, fusing conventionality with a deconstructive postmodernity. Perhaps it is, indeed, art cinema, just not in the way one would expect. Seoul, for example, is at times utilised as an intensely familiar space. We can clearly recognise specific areas, buildings and even people. Yet, even amongst this familiarity there is a pervading ambivalence, a sense of deeper symbolism and meaning embedded within a typical urban façade. If we are to draw parallels between the depiction of Seoul and Korean identity in general, which on many different occasions *3-Iron* suggests and requires that we do, there seems to be much more at stake when considering the 'self' and how it is conditioned by a greater exterior force. Whether it is concerning identity, narrative or character, the unconventional always resides *within* the conventional, and the imaginary *within* the 'real'. By foregrounding these juxtapositions, or collisions, the film is enforcing their importance not simply within its own fantastical story but also in relation to a wider, and significantly more complex, Korean social narrative.

References

Anderson, B. 2006. *Imagined Communities: Reflections on the Origin and Spread of Nationalism*, Revised Edition. London: Verso.
Bhabha, H. 1994. *The Localization of Culture*. New York: Routledge.
Cardullo, B. 2007. Back to the Future, or the Vanguard Meets the Rearguard. *Jump Cut: A Review of Contemporary Media* 49 (page numbers not available).
Cho, M. 1999. Flexible Sociality and the Postmodernity of Seoul. *Korea Journal* 39 (3): 122–142.
Chung, H. 2010. Beyond Extreme: Rereading Kim Ki-Duk's Cinema of Ressentiment. *Journal of Film and Video* 62 (1): 96–11. https://doi.org/10.1353/jfv.0.0054.
Jin, D. 2010. Critical Interpretation of Hybridisation in Korean Cinema: Does the local film industry create 'The Third Space'? *Javnost-The Public* 17 (1): 55–71. https://doi.org/10.1080/13183222.2010.11009026.
Joo, J. 2011. Transnationalization of Korean Popular Culture and the Rise of Pop Nationalism in Korea. *Journal of Popular Culture* 44 (3): 489–504. https://doi.org/10.1111/j.1540-5931.2011.00845.x.
Kim, Y. 2004. Seoul: Complimenting Economic Success with Games. In *World Cities Beyond the West: Globalization, Development and Inequality*, ed. Josef Gugler, 59–81. Cambridge: Cambridge University Press.
Kim, S. 2014. Mirror Play, or Subjectivization in *3 Iron*: Based on Lacan's Analysis of *Les Meninas* and his Optical Model. *Acta Koreana* 17 (1): 105–135. https://doi.org/10.18399/acta.2014.17.1.005.
Lacan, J. 2004. The Mirror Stage as Formative of the Function of the I as Revealed in Psychoanalytic Experience. In *Literary Theory: An Anthology*, ed. Julie Rivkin and Michael Ryan, 2nd ed. Oxford: Wiley-Blackwell.
Maltby, R. 2003. *Hollywood Cinema*. 2nd ed. Oxford: Wiley-Blackwell.
Marshall, C. 2017. Lacking in Seoul? Why South Korea's Thriving Capital is Having an Identity Crisis. *The Guardian*. Accessed 21 January 2018. https://

www.theguardian.com/cities/2017/jul/18/seoul-south-korea-identity-crisis-brand-psy-gangnam-style.

Mennel, B. 2008. *Cities and Cinema: Routledge Critical Introductions to Urbanism and the City*. London; New York: Routledge.

Shin, C., and J. Stringer. 2007. Storming the Big Screen: The *Shiri* Syndrome. In *Seoul Searching: Culture and Identity in Contemporary Korean Cinema*, ed. Frances Gateward, 55–69. New York: State University of New York Press.

Soja, E. 1996. *Thirdspace: Journeys to Los Angeles and Other Real-And-Imagined Places*. Oxford: Wiley-Blackwell.

Tajbakhsh, K. 2001. *The Promise of the City: Space, Identity and Politics in Contemporary Social Thought*. Berkley, California: University of California Press.

Yacowar, M. 2000. The City in Cinema. *Queen's Quarterly* 107 (2): 273–283.

CHAPTER 3

The Generic City

On 13 February 1999, director Kang Je-Gyu's action-packed *Shiri* was released in cinemas across South Korea. The praise it received at the time established a turning point for the industry and its future creators, particularly because it was one of the first successful products conceived during a period of major economic growth within the country. This meant that *Shiri*, and the industry in which it was made, gained international traction in a short space of time and were soon recognised as indicators of, and valued additions to, the nation's positive economic incline. More importantly, however, the film marked South Korea's introductory venture into big-budget cinematic production and thus solidified the new era or 'wave' of Korean national filmmaking.

Evidently, the film certainly fits the 'blockbuster' criteria—that is, it seemingly resembles the *Hollywood* conception of such, especially when comparing it to the male-driven, action-oriented, highly energised and efficient narratives of the 1980s. The appropriation of a seemingly generic, and therefore accessible, 'model' inevitably contributed towards the film's instantaneous notability. It proved to be a financial, cultural and global success, insofar that it inaugurated a period thereafter in which Korean films were acknowledged on a much broader, international and competitive scale. For the Korean national audience, meanwhile, *Shiri's* popularity quickly eclipsed that of James Cameron's *Titanic* (1997), a significant feat

© The Author(s), under exclusive license to Springer Nature Switzerland AG 2023
G. Ballard, *Urban Landscapes and National Visions in Post-Millennial South Korean Cinema*, East Asian Popular Culture, https://doi.org/10.1007/978-3-031-29739-7_3

for a film that, by comparison, cost significantly less to make. As Ryoo Woongjae observes, from the 1990s to the present, 'South Korea is one of the few countries where Hollywood productions do not enjoy a dominant share of the domestic market', and *Shiri* still exists as the primary reference point for, and instigator of, this economic trend (Ryoo 2009, p. 141). Therefore, if the American counterpart cannot compete, one has to question why exactly Korean texts like *Shiri*, when ostensibly patterned on a universally recognisable 'blockbuster' framework, continue to dominate.

The film follows South Korean special agent Yu Jongwon and his ill-fated partner Lee Jangil as they attempt to rid Seoul of infiltrators and spies from the enemy North. More specifically, they are searching for an elite female sniper named Bang Hee, who at the beginning of the film has already assassinated several prominent South Korean figures and government officials, and as such, has deeply compromised the political landscape. From this description alone, it is already clear why this text initiates a process of structural, stylistic and thematic oscillation, particularly with regard to the conventional blockbuster and its primary cinematic occupation. A level of cultural and political specificity is apparent here, designed to accommodate and satisfy a largely *national* audience. *Shiri's* story concerns itself with a distinctively national and contemporary anxiety: the threat of North Korea and its potential presence within the expanding and diversifying city of Seoul. Through the focalisation of a culturally and socially exclusive narrative, *Shiri* effectively 'Koreanises' its own (ostensibly) generic template.

At the turn of the Twenty-first century, integration, cooperation and 'constructive engagement policies' occupied a significant space in South Korea's political, social and national consciousness (Levin and Han 2002, p. 23). The 'Sunshine Policy', introduced in 1998 during the administration of Kim Dae-Jung, was indicative of a broader, outward-facing, diplomatic move to help improve the relationship between the two Koreas and stagnate any potential military threat. However, many of the approaches embedded within this new agenda only served to intensify 'long-standing, unresolved societal tensions and divisions' and, more importantly, emphasise national differences (Levin and Han 2002, p. 31). There was an apparent disparity between the superficial, external purpose of the policy and its internal goals. Above all else, the policy was met with some criticism from a public that had been significantly shaped by years of intermittent national trauma and periods of systemic change. Questions concerning future relations, economic impact and diplomatic engagement were inextricably tied to what is now viewed as a significant shift in the South Korean governmental approach to North Korea.

While there may be just cause to reevaluate the impact of the 'Sunshine Policy' (to determine whether it was, indeed, a success or failure), such pursuits are perhaps better reserved for a more politically focused study. I would, however, argue that the policy served to heighten the awareness of North/South relations, and in doing so facilitated new cultural narratives, interests and objectives—many of which are highlighted in South Korean cinema of the millennial era. Despite (or maybe even because of) its blockbuster exterior, *Shiri* magnifies the national concerns of the period and the anxieties surrounding initiatives akin to the 'Sunshine Policy'. Even as it attempts to show the changing and ambivalent relationship between North and South Korea, there is the suggestion that the status quo is something to be preserved—that is, a continued acknowledgement of the division. Prior to the very first scene, a written passage appears on screen reminding us of the division between the 'communistic North' and the 'democratic South'. It also affirms that the two nations remain 'under the state of suspended war', in which 'tension runs high even at this very moment'. The summary is simple and concise, and sets an anticipatory tone for the film. There is an immediacy and urgency with which *Shiri* establishes the intense social and political landscape, and this ultimately demonstrates a desire for national relevance and cultural exactitude. Fundamentally, this initial statement operates as an emphatic address of a singular and highly isolated conflict—a subject that is deeply embedded within Korea's collective national consciousness. As a consequence, this brief, pre-emptive passage significantly alters how we watch, absorb and ultimately 'read' the film (be it from a domestic or international viewpoint).

Shortly after the opening message, a brutal training montage ensues and largely focuses on the ruthless Bang Hee, who excels far beyond her inferior male counterparts. Ordinarily, one would view this scene as a standard feature of action cinema. It operates as an energetic, ultra-violent and dynamic introduction to a key character and, more importantly, establishes a level of 'movie spectacle'. To a certain extent, the sequence will always function in this conventional way—it works as a successful amalgamation of high-budget visuals and effectual narrative markers. Size, scale and technical ambition are made obvious from the early stages of the film. With the knowledge of certain events, however, provided by the aforementioned preceding statement, this training montage adopts a much darker and sinister meaning. We are thus burdened by our own extra-textual, 'exterior' knowledge of the complex, hyper-political landscape in which the film takes place. Evidently, even the most conventional of sequences have been 'indigenised' or 'injected with local concerns and local subject matter' in this South Korean incarnation of the blockbuster, as Julian Stringer observes (Stringer 2010, p. 59). Therefore, in this particular instance, Bang Hee's entry remains tainted with a touch of 'real' anxiety, threat and potential danger. There is a duality and complexity of meaning embedded within this opening scene, which greatly compromises our pre-conceived idea of the blockbuster and the audience for whom this seemingly familiar text is supposedly intended.

The depiction of the city is, once again, instrumental to this process, as the modification or deflection of the expectations manifested by the national audience begins with, and is crystallised within, the Seoul landscape. Every sustained action sequence in *Shiri* takes place within, and is interrupted by, an inimitable Korean setting and its array of multifaceted voices and/or identities. This is further emphasised by the fact that most of the film is shot on location, in and amongst the streets and citizens of the capital city, Seoul. During a chase sequence, in which Yu Jongwon and Lee Jangil pursue an arms dealer (with potential information about the enemy North), the film rapidly transports the audience from one urban setting to another. A variety of Korean workers, shoppers, school students and tourists enter in and leave the frame, providing a fleeting glimpse of contemporary Korean existence. At the same time, however, there are also continuous allusions to the North/South conflict, which are manifested within the diegetic space both visually and aurally. The communal and commonplace areas in which the chase takes place are also indicative of this.

Before having recognised their target, the characters walk through a bustling supermarket. The 'customer announcements' that one would expect to hear in this environment feature throughout, but they are occasionally intermingled with updates about the current political climate and/or the conflict with North Korea. We are told that a 'friendly' football match between the two states is about to take place and will provide further support towards 'peace negotiations'. The statement is haunting as it appears contemptuous and hopeful in equal measure, largely due to the self-conscious, cynical and darkly humorous construction of the scene itself. Just as the words are spoken, Bang Hee appears in the background, behind an oblivious Yu Jongwon. She clearly represents the antithetical counterpart to 'peace', and her presence in the frame greatly compromises the supposed stability of the public space. *Shiri* is clearly commenting on the promise (or futility) of 'progress' here by emphasising the vulnerability of both the landscape and the many identities that live within it and rely upon it.

The impact of war and its influence are made apparent within all factions of Korean society. There is the persistent sense that this is no 'ordinary' conflict. *Shiri* is addressing a present, ongoing and intensely topical crisis, which demonstrates a significant divergence from Western form. The Hollywood blockbuster, by comparison, has often been characterised by its persistent level of 'conscience liberalism', whereby any political/social/historical commentary is often marginalised by aspects of convention (Maltby 2003). One rarely expects the blockbuster to sustain a level of topical enquiry. Certain questions can be raised of course, or issues introduced, but they are seldom explored in their entirety or directly confronted by the narrative itself. *Shiri*, on the other hand, seeks to illuminate its own political discourse by drawing close attention to the impact of war on every area within the diegesis.

This is not to say, however, that the film uses its inherently cultural narrative to mitigate its attachment to the predetermined expectations of the blockbuster text. On the contrary, it recognises the importance of adhering to a conventional formula and utilises the patterns embedded within this structure to further spectacularise its own narrative (and maintain a crucial level of accessibility). There is clearly a sense of formal recognition here (particularly when considering the obligatory tropes of popular cinema), but it never fully unfolds into a *reliance* on the 'Western way'. While the foundations of the blockbuster model are certainly present, they are not used to dictate the overall presentation and, more importantly, the meaning of the finished product. These remain in a strict realm of Korean authority. It is therefore worth questioning the fundamentals of the blockbuster itself and its stylistic mutability when it is relocated in other national cinemas. In order to achieve this, we must start by looking at the industry in which it was initially conceived and the key factors behind its continued success.

Adoption and Inheritance: The Question of Cinematic Ownership

The meaning of the term 'blockbuster' has diversified considerably over the last 40 years. In its infancy, it was primarily thought of as a lucrative Hollywood production, a functional commodity and, above all else, a mode and product synonymous with a specific phase of post-classical 'studio' filmmaking. To a certain extent, these characteristics remain applicable to modern blockbusters and have been sustained by the expectations of both the audiences who watch them and the industries that create them. In retrospect, however, and by looking at the cinematic timeline of the blockbuster in its entirety, our former ideas about this recognisable product and its function have significantly altered, particularly when considered alongside, and within, other national cinemas. *Shiri* is particularly important when observing this textual development and its overall cinematic impact.

To observe these changes, nevertheless, one must start at the beginning and identify the basic foundations of the standard blockbuster framework. Fundamentally, the *Hollywood* blockbuster is still associated with large-scale filmmaking and is designed to incorporate all the technological potential of cinema. Our understanding of such has been largely shaped by the 'New Hollywood' period, with films by directors such as Steven Spielberg and George Lucas igniting the industry's desire to fuse big-budget production (and, latterly, film experimentation) with an ostensibly classical narrative. One should also acknowledge how the 'blockbuster' often connotes the studio 'movie', as opposed to the 'film', as it is commonly assumed that the former is a commercially driven product designed for international appeal (and must, therefore, be globally distributed). Such texts are intended to be spectacular and accessible to the diverse masses. They promise thrilling peril, adventure and fantasy, where ordinary characters are likely to find themselves in the most extraordinary of circumstances.

There is a sense of grand universal appeal embedded within these films and, as Julian Stringer states, an inherent sense of 'size', which is a 'central notion through which the blockbuster's generic identity comes to be identified' (Stringer 2003, p. 3). Most importantly, however, the blockbuster story-model is understood and defined in terms of its linear, coherent and consistent framework—a strict 'cause and effect' structure that concludes with a clear sense of resolution and narrative equilibrium. Main characters, meanwhile, are expected to be stable, reliable and above all else, figures with whom the audience can empathise and use to navigate the diegetic space. As spectators of the blockbuster, we seldom expect to be challenged by its narrative or to occupy an 'active' role in deciphering the events depicted on screen. The film often does the work for us, so we can absorb the story in a relatively passive manner.

Even though there are, of course, strong exceptions to these rules, the (Hollywood) blockbuster is predominantly viewed as a conventional cinematic piece and has over the years grown susceptible to the same kind of standardisation as many other recognisable genres. There will always be key signifiers (embedded within foundational semiotic approaches) that allow us to differentiate a blockbuster from an art-house film, for example, as well as intrinsic expectations that perpetuate these general readerly approaches. While one cannot underestimate the practicality and efficiency of these methods, it is always important to recognise the texts that defy the equation and question how and why this has been achieved. If the accuracy of the common theories and assumptions made about the blockbuster are to be further interrogated, it is important to begin by dissecting its seemingly inextricable relationship to Hollywood. This not only provides space to rethink the established parallels and paradigms that exist between American filmmaking and popular cinema, but it also allows the freedom to 'place' the blockbuster on a much broader, global spectrum—and remove it from the Western foundations upon which it was originally devised. Whilst regarded as intrinsic to modern American film practice, the blockbuster is no longer exclusive to Hollywood. It has become a universalised and accessible form of film language, as well as an adaptable discourse that can easily exist within, and be moulded by, any cultural and historical framework—*Shiri* is clearly indicative of this international and intertextual premise. I would argue that, more so than any other film form, the blockbuster is most susceptible to a positive process of nationalisation. Its journey from infancy has been marked by a significant degree of transformation, stylistic rejuvenation and cinematic evolution from other world industries. Even with these cinematic mutations, nevertheless, the connotations to Hollywood remain unwavering and, for understandable reasons, are impossible to evade when observing the ways in which the conventions of popular film are integrated and later presented in other national cinemas, particularly in East Asia.

Darcy Paquet argues that in South Korea especially, 'the meaning of the term blockbuster ... has evolved over time', and whilst there have been attempts to 'de-westernise' the genre, 'Korean filmmakers' appropriation of the blockbuster model [remains] a topic of intense debate' (Paquet 2009, pp. 74–75). This argument, and in particular the use of the term 'appropriation', not only draws attention to a self-perpetuating sequence of borrowing, repeating and reconditioning but also infers a lack of artistic faithfulness and originality within the industry (with regard to big-budget productions). Having looked at the structure of *Shiri*, it would be incorrect to assume modern Korean cinema has in no part been influenced by the filmic endeavours of Hollywood or persuaded by the commercial success and high consumption of the industry's blockbuster releases.

Spectacle, adventure and an escapist narrative promise mass audiences and large profits, and South Korea has certainly capitalised on this in recent years, particularly as a response to the 'cinephilia' or 'cine-mania' that is currently sweeping the country, as Kim So-Young defines (Kim 2005, p. 79). However, to argue that the country's 'version' of the blockbuster exists only as a reproduction or copy of the standard American model is too simplistic and premature a conclusion to reach. While the connections are fairly clear in some cases, with regard to generic expectations and paradigms, the South Korean film industry has sought to individualise and differentiate its own discourse in order to create and maintain a national cinematic voice not only within independent projects but also in larger studio productions. Jinhee Choi believes one must distinguish the 'Korean blockbuster' from 'the Hollywood conception of blockbuster movies', as the former demands 'a different set of measures in order to be properly situated and evaluated' (Choi 2010, pp. 31–32). Here, Choi suggests that not only is it difficult to approach Korean popular film in the same way we would American, or any other kind of world cinema for that matter, there is also the sense that it would be inherently wrong to do so. This is because there is a wealth of distinctive and unique contextual factors to consider, many of which do not immediately apply to Hollywood and/or the West. By focusing on Korean culture and identity (and questioning the extent to which these facets are incorporated into the familiar narratives of popular cinema), the comparisons with Hollywood's hegemonic authority, though apparent to an extent, certainly hold less significance and formal gravity.

Evidently, stylistic hybridisation, which refers to the overlapping of different film discourses and techniques, has proved to be a largely successful exercise for the South Korean film industry. Recent statistics show that the most commercially successful films made, distributed and released in South Korea (post-*Shiri*) are typically classified as 'blockbusters'; their spectacle, budget and positive domestic reception having eclipsed overseas competition.[1] Thus, Korean audiences are clearly drawn to their own cultural narratives, irrespective of the manner in which they are manufactured, packaged and eventually 'sold'. There is clearly a desire to have one's own national identity displayed on an expansive platform—the cinema screen—and more importantly to have this realised in a way that is both entertaining and culturally faithful. This means that even the familiar blockbuster can be perceived as an entirely independent and distinctive Korean creation, from production to exhibition. These films are largely financed by *Korean* studios. They are the collective creations of *Korean* directors, producers, writers and cinematographers, who employ *Korean* stars to deliver their *Korean* stories.

Marco Cucco maintains that the blockbuster is a 'transnational product', which means it is 'designed for commercial utilization on the global market' (Cucco 2009, p. 217). While this appears to be true with regard to how the blockbuster concept is adopted and promoted, Cucco also claims that this process has resulted in the 'loss of cultural specificity' (Cucco 2009). This suggests that the blockbuster exists only as a generalised film product, absent of any specific identity (hence, ownership), and is therefore easily transferable between different world cinemas. The South Korean film industry, on the other hand, seems to provide a strong point of contention to this argument, as with every big-budget release there appears to be an intentional desire to move away from the standard blockbuster 'model' and instead create something distinctively and inherently national. This can be achieved in various ways, as identified within *Shiri*. It can occur through the subversion of genre, the inclusion of familiar Korean characters and social narratives or, as is the case most recently, the engagement with a recognisable part of Korean history (especially the North/South divide, the colonial era and/or the Japanese occupation). Utilising the paradigmatic structure of the blockbuster, or any form of popular cinema for that matter, does not necessarily mean that cultural specificity is sacrificed or 'lost' in favour of generic modes of story-telling. The standard and conventional foundations clearly exist, but the finished product is by no means interchangeable or replicable. South Korea's box office is indicative of this, as it is continuously dominated by its own

---

[1] Box Office by Year, data provided by the *Korean Film Council*. www.kobis.or.uk. Accessed 16th July 2018.

domestic productions, no matter how big or small. This demonstrates a current collective yearning to preserve a distinctively national narrative, both on and off the cinema screen.

Not only is the question of social, cultural and historical identity of paramount concern for many Korean films, including the blockbuster, but it is also embedded within the expectations of the audiences who watch them. More importantly, however, this deeply intertwined relationship between reader and text validates a highly unique concern that arguably relates to South Korea *alone,* which suggests that, contrary to Cucco's argument, cultural specificity can never be entirely diminished when there are national anxieties and questions yet to be remedied or satisfied. South Korea is still, at this very moment, living through the repercussions and ramifications of its own recent history, and this has produced a public that is still, to a large extent, in a state of flux. As such, popular cultural productions are responsible not only for addressing these national fluctuations and narratives, but they also contribute to the very shaping and definition of this recent history.

All of which implies that even the ostensibly 'generic' blockbuster can carry a certain amount of figurative and artistic weight, as is evidenced within various Korean films throughout the post-millennial period—many of which have achieved notable critical attention from domestic and international spectators. From the 1990s to the present, this emphatic remodelling of genre discourses and patterns (via the integration of collective social narrative and specific cultural paradigms) has somewhat mitigated the effects of 'Hollywood domination', as Seung Hyun Park describes, mainly because Korean filmmakers have now 'realised film's value … as an entertainment commodity and as a medium for symbolic expression' (Park 2007, p. 31). Bong Joon Ho's *The Host* (2006) is also indicative of this and, like *Shiri*, is another South Korean blockbuster text that is at once familiar to a local audience, yet decidedly unfamiliar to an international one.

Monster Metropolis: Ambivalent Conventionality in Korean Blockbuster Horror

From analysis of the most recent and lucrative South Korean productions, an immediate and topical understanding of the industry's contemporary aesthetic can be discerned. Within this modern style, the features of its own cinematic timeline (in addition to those of other national cinemas) can also be identified. The evolving interests of contemporary Korean audiences and their film habits may also become more evident when studying such texts. Following *Shiri*, the next South Korean 'blockbuster' to break box office records and receive worldwide recognition was, indeed, *The Host*. Though there had been other notable texts released in the six years that separated these two films, none could compare to the financial and technological heights of director Bong's third feature. As such, *The Host* marked another significant 'phase' of Korean national filmmaking. More importantly, it introduced a new cinematic trend—'big-budget horror'. By acknowledging and incorporating the popular aesthetic of its predecessors, namely *Shiri*, *The Host* had an established platform on which to build and experiment. The locally altered parameters of genre and character thus became a primary focus for further interrogation within the film.

Darcy Paquet argues that the family at the centre of the narrative is integral to the culturally conscientious nature of the film as 'each character may be seen as representing a different decade of Korean history' (Paquet 2009, p. 106). Out of the many films released within the late Twentieth and early Twenty-first century 'boom' period of Korean filmmaking, no text has received quite the same level of global recognition as *The Host* (apart from perhaps Park Chan Wook's *Oldboy*). In particular, the film has received a significant level of concentrated academic focus, most likely because, as Paquet continues, it 'represents the final maturation of Korean cinema from a weak, highly regulated industry ... to a competitive, globalized business' (Paquet, p. 108). This is not to say, however, that it is now a redundant exercise to analyse *The Host*. Even with a wealth of readings and textual interpretations already undertaken, the scale of the film's impact, legacy and national significance demands further elucidation. Not only did it celebrate a significant transition between old and new styles of national filmmaking, but it was arguably the first 'big-budget' film that invited a profound international response, even more so than *Shiri* (which is still, as previously mentioned, considered to be the country's introductory 'blockbuster' production).

Regardless of this global engagement and accessibility, the film remains an exclusively Korean text as it endeavours to sustain cultural specificity and thus appeal to a domestic audience. The story follows the destructive actions of a giant fish-like creature, a mutant of sorts, which is the result of the careless disposal of toxic waste into Seoul's sewer and drainage system. Eventually, the film takes the audience to the heart of the city, the Han River, where the monster resides and claims its first victims. By initially shooting on location and using such a distinctive, recognisable and ultimately 'real' South Korean landmark, the text immediately establishes its own Korean identity and in doing so celebrates the country's inimitable urban landscape. Seoul is presented as a highly mappable cinematic space—it follows a structural and functional pattern, and our position within the diegetic world is always made plain as a result. The Han River stands at the centre of this postmodern vista. It is a fixture that connects the different factions of the urban landscape and, more importantly, acts as a foundation from which all narratives are born and later dependent upon.

The Host is considered to be a highly valuable contribution to South Korea's 'Renaissance' period of filmmaking (which concerns productions from the late 1990s to the present), as well as a fundamental illustration of the new 'Korean blockbuster'. Christina Klein argues that the text exemplifies the industry's 'ambivalent' relationship with Hollywood, as it 'subverts genre conventions even as [it] evokes them', while simultaneously following a recognisable 'structural template'—which, in this instance, refers to narrative linearity, efficiency and coherency (Klein 2008, p. 886). The domestic and international attention the film garnered upon its release may be attributed to this simultaneous acknowledgement and disturbance of popular form and style, particularly when considering the function of the 'monster'. The creature of *The Host* acts more as a vehicle or catalyst for character development as opposed to a fixture of permanent threat and spectacle. After the introductory scene of destruction, it is very rarely seen in its entirety. When incompetent father Gang-Du witnesses the monster 'take' his daughter during the first few moments of the film, a close-up of his horrified face occupies the majority of the short sequence, as opposed to the horrifying act itself. The delayed revelation of events forces the viewer to rely on the expression of the character alone and emphasises the chaotic gravity of what is presumably happening off camera. It immediately becomes apparent that, as spectators, the film is manipulating our attention, persuading us to momentarily overlook the physical presence of the monster and, indeed, relinquish our own expectations. Thus, focus is once again realigned and positioned solely on the 'ordinary'—the dysfunctional, yet wholly sympathetic, Korean family (and this presentation is fully facilitated by the presentation of the highly specific urban landscape in which the characters collectively live, work and exist). It is at this point that the nature of 'Koreanness' is fully established within the film.

The scene of collective mourning, which takes places shortly after the first attack, is largely indicative of this. With television cameras present, the family comes together to grieve in a formal ceremony, alongside many others who have lost loved ones to the monster. The film's focalisation of this subversive nuclear unit draws attention to an inimitable Korean narrative. Unlike the rest of the mourners, who are either wearing traditional funeral attire or black suits, Gang-du and his father arrive in the same clothes they were wearing during the attack—casual, informal tracksuits now stained with dirt and blood, their hair laden with sweat. When the other family members arrive, the grief they all share overwhelms them as they collapse to the ground, fall onto one another and descend into a fit of bellowing cries. The scene is highly humorous, uncomfortable and surprising in equal measures (and thus further subverts any representational norms). This outburst is met, meanwhile, with the slightly bemused and judgemental stares of various onlookers, as well as a plethora of jarring camera flashes. The camera is positioned directly above the family and forces us to look down on the chaotic and uninhibited display, which perhaps acts as a subtle stylistic mirroring of the views and attitudes of those who surround them. A sense of social division is immediately made apparent.

While this is an obvious representation of Korean identity, it is not necessarily the one we would expect (particularly within this kind of text). One has the impression that even though these working Korean citizens are by no means 'poor', Seoul's social, cultural and economic 'boom' has somehow bypassed them, and the film is determined to make this clear. This is a highly personal narrative, as it deliberately attempts to erase the global orchestration of South Korea's image, as well as the 'bigger picture' of Seoul—that of an economically successful state that benefits every city dweller. In this instance, the 'Korean Blockbuster', a product of this 'new' landscape, seeks to deconstruct its own capitalist properties. We are thus provided with a much more intimate portrait of Korean sensibility and of the 'regular' Seoulite, which includes everyday hardships, family conflicts and financial quarrels. The obligatory action and spectacle of such texts, whilst not drawing direct attention to these issues, in no way marginalises them either.

The fact that these characters and livelihoods are recognised by *The Host* remains a positive feature because, as Nikki Lee summarises, 'using a family-centred drama ensures that the film appeals to audiences of multiple generations', and more importantly, speaks directly to a Korean spectatorship (Lee 2011, p. 54). This suggests that, in film especially, the fundamental characteristics, movement and expansion of the Korean audience are used to inform the overarching presentation of national identity on screen. Timeliness is therefore key to the *The Host's* success. The film not only references a specific point in the country's post-millennial timeline (the period soon after the economic 'boom'), but it also questions its lasting impact, or lack of, on a certain kind of Korean identity (via Gang-Du and his family). Their condition is linked to a specific window of time in contemporary South Korean history—the 'era' that follows a landmark financial, social and cultural shift. For the Korean audiences that watched the film when it was initially released, their extra-textual awareness and knowledge of the changing landscape at the time would have greatly altered how they viewed and engaged with the text—particularly for those who may have also experienced the negative impact of the 1997 International Monetary Fund (IMF) crisis. To be able to acutely identify with the characters and the world in which they live, work and co-exist is a reader/text privilege that remains exclusive to the domestic audience alone. This intimate celluloid dialogue cannot be achieved elsewhere. *The Host's* emphatic depiction of Korean archetypes, unique time periods and factions of Korean society is indicative of the manner in which this 'connection' is sustained. Essentially, the characters in the film have a greater function than the standard horror text often permits—they illuminate the *Korean* experience in what might still be perceived as an internationally accessible text.

Yeon Sang Ho's recent zombie horror *Train to Busan* (2016) works in the same way and, like *The Host*, demonstrates the tempestuous relationship between, and problematic readings of, Eastern and Western filmmaking. It uses its characters to simultaneously evoke and destabilise the expectations of popular cinema (inaugurated by Hollywood) and the genre to which it seemingly belongs. Yet, the film remains fundamentally accessible, understandable and enjoyable for both national and international audiences alike. *Train to Busan's* unique and self-reflexive approach to style and form is largely responsible for this. While its narrative structure satisfies the generic 'category' with which it is ostensibly associated, the various levels of self-reflexivity embedded within its presentation complicate the supposed conventionality of the story, which demonstrates, as David S. Diffrient summarises, 'the industry's millennial drive towards genre diversification' (Diffrient 2003, pp. 60–71).

While *The Host* questions the 'rules' or limitations of genre, *Train to Busan* seeks to undermine its textual authority altogether. Indeed, despite it being labelled as an 'action-horror', the film's treatment of the tropes associated with the genre often verge (intentionally) on the comedic, and even the parodic. The 'scares' are certainly present, but they are laced with a perpetually self-deprecating quality, and there are constant reminders to both the audience and the characters of the frenetic absurdity rooted within certain situations. Other recent horror films have also incorporated a sense of dark comedy and have proved incredibly popular with audiences. *Chaw* (2009), *Spellbound* (2011) and *Ghost Sweepers* (2012) are just a few examples of South Korean texts that fuse elements of genuine horror, even terror, and an unexpected level of comedy. Not only is this suggestive of an inherent postmodernity and intertextuality, but it also shows a willingness to reevaluate the conventions of the horror narrative alongside the aforementioned expectations of its dominant viewership. This is particularly the case for the expectations found within, and sustained by, the Hollywood spectator (which largely concern generic rigidity and consistency). *The Host* and *Train to Busan*, meanwhile, demonstrate the permeability of genre and how it can expand far beyond its classical parameters and/or signifiers.

Even though one might describe it as an ensemble piece, *Train to Busan*'s story largely focuses on the efforts of one man as he tries to negotiate relentless attacks from the 'infected' (humans that have been afflicted by an unknown disease), all while attempting to get his daughter to safety. Most of the action is contained and takes place on a train from Seoul to Busan, with a small group of passengers that, like father and daughter, have also managed to escape the growing epidemic. However, it eventually becomes clear that the characters on board must face the threat not only from the infected but also from each other, as tensions and the human will to survive inevitably take precedence. Again, with clear elements of horror and comedy (the latter of which explicitly accommodates Korean audiences and their cultural sensibilities), the film appears to challenge the pre-conceived assumptions made about the blockbuster. These moments of tonal hybridity arrive during the most unexpected moments and are often used to speak directly to a domestic spectator.

After a graphic fight sequence, during which a mobile phone is used to distract the 'infected', a comment on the 'tackiness' of the ringtone (a popular and traditional Korean 'trot' song) immediately interrupts what may have otherwise evolved into a dramatic monologue. Narrative exposition is at once developed and amusingly thwarted, spectacle is momentarily halted by a subversive critique of the mundane and the boundaries of the story-world, whilst still certainly intact, are greatly challenged in this moment. The film knowingly draws attention to its own 'celluloid' qualities, as well as a temporal vulnerability, by occasionally positioning the characters within a separate space or meta-narrative in which they too are aware of their filmic properties and their 'movie-like' situation. As a result, the diegesis is regularly disturbed or humorously disrupted. Thus, the expectations of the horror genre are met with an equal sense of affection and cynicism. This is not to say, however, that *Train to Busan* completely evades or reworks the stereotypical features of the standard horror text. It only suggests that it occasionally meets these tropes with a certain amount of flexibility, especially when regarding how such paradigms are presented on screen or delivered to the audience.

The film is permeated by countless intertextual projections and cinematic clones; a typically 'evil' antagonist, a young child designed to strike empathy within the audience, flawed familial relationships, isolated moments of action or suspense, a sacrificial character that evokes a sense of loss ... the list is comprehensive. While this constant recycling of the 'generic' further stabilises conventional and commercial engagement, the way in which the reproductions are persistently recognised demonstrates a perverse level of self-consciousness. Evidently, the characters in *Train to Busan* initially appear hyperbolic and one-dimensional, presented in a manner that seems almost caricature. They are instantly recognisable beings, seemingly formulaic in both delivery and purpose.

As the narrative develops, however, and chaos intensifies, it becomes clear that this diverse ensemble is not simply a group that can be exchanged for any other, despite the film's introductory characterisation. These people are clearly 'Seoulites' (as are those in *The Host*). They act as reflections and representations of the increasingly hybridised communities that exist alongside one another in South Korea's expansive capital city. They are constructed as products of a specifically *Korean* urban environment—different generations that each signify conflicting national realities, and the separate stages of Seoul's rapid growth and development. This means that the city lives *within* them—it informs their own existence and determines their place within the filmic world. Therefore, Seoul is always present on screen, even if we cannot see it physically. It is persistently filtered through these distinctive characters and further illuminated in the urban and/or Korean demographics they represent. Just as the family in *The Host* draw attention to a unique point in time and place, the diverse group of passengers in *Train to Busan* are equally symptomatic of an increasingly modernised, present-day Korea—they represent the Seoul of 'today'.

The emphatic shift of the narrative 'spotlight' in both texts not only demonstrates a level of localisation (as each film prioritises the collective actions of the typical Korean family or citizen in the face of disaster, loss and spectacle) but also a reconfiguration of the expectations associated with the 'monster' genre—namely that the 'monster' itself is marginalised by a specific cultural storyline. *The Host* in particular seems to take this further given that the monster is very seldom seen as a 'complete' threat, physically and symbolically. It is only a secondary component within the diegetic world, which is not something one would typically anticipate from a film categorised as a 'horror blockbuster'. The physical absence of the creature, however, ensures that the film is enabled space for defamiliarisation and innovation, and is therefore more likely to destabilise certain genre tropes or challenge the binaries of horror (and Hollywood) story-telling.

Where one obligatory trope is missing, a new and unconventional approach is soon ready to replace it, and it is often socially, culturally and historically relevant. Here again, we are able to distinguish the 'Korean blockbuster' from a more general understanding of the term/concept, primarily because the attention towards an identifiable social facet of the national landscape speaks to a singularly South Korean viewership. While such films can be consumed and appreciated by any spectator, as is perhaps the primary goal of the blockbuster, these texts are clearly intended to satisfy the expectations of a highly specific, culturally unique and socially independent demographic—and their domestic success is a testament to this fact.

In cases such as these, it appears that the concept of Korean national identity is continually foregrounded, alongside its relationship with, and position within, an increasingly urbanised social landscape. Like many other post-millennial blockbusters, *The Host* stresses the absolute interconnectedness between the leading characters and an intensifying urbanity as, similarly to the passengers in *Train to Busan*, each family member embodies a specific phase of Seoul's commercial, economic and cultural progress. Perhaps more important, however, is the emphasis on an intergenerational group of protagonists, all of whom contribute towards South Korea's hybridised and inclusive national consciousness. There is a certain element of history to be found and sustained within every contemporary piece here (albeit in a fairly idiosyncratic way) and a shared acknowledgement of Seoul's turbulent past alongside the complex journey of every citizen (who has, on any level, been a part of it).

The notion of the urban self, therefore, is not necessarily limited to the modern or the 'new'. It is instead an adaptable discourse that can exist within, and be inherited by, each 'variation' of Korean identity. Thus, the critical understanding that urban existence helps to create and sustain a stagnant postmodernity is once again challenged by a unique Korean desire to preserve and evolve the social, cultural and historical 'self' (which links back to *3-Iron's* engagement with performativity and self-determined identity construction). Despite the apparent modernity, thrill and sheer entertainment value of *Shiri, The Host* and *Train to Busan,* which they all clearly have in abundance, their narratives remain greatly concerned with the longevity of Korean identity, as well as the conservation of a nationally recognised and culturally inimitable Seoul. The only way that this can truly be achieved, however, is through the continued integration of *historical* narratives, whether stylistically, figuratively or emotionally.

The evocation of the past, and its persistent impact on contemporary Korean existence, is paramount to the country's collective 'narrative' and identity. The Korean film industry remains forever aware of this. Even though it constantly works towards global recognition and a general sense of cinematic 'newness', it simultaneously acknowledges the cultural importance of previous narratives, conflicts, landscapes and, above all, identities. A process of nationalisation is clearly evident here, captured by the industry's collective need to sustain a temporal textuality within its own multi-faceted discourse. The conscious overlapping or hybridisation of time means that aspects of Korean national history are evident within even the most contemporary of texts—including the blockbuster. This is the point at which South Korean popular cinema, in its many forms, decidedly separates itself from Hollywood, from other East Asian cinemas and, most importantly, from the established expectations of the genre.

Society on Screen: Magnifying Urban 'Reality'

The Host and *Train to Busan* establish every character as a valid and instrumental facet of the story-world, and it is made clear that these constructions epitomise certain aspects of the Korean social landscape. In the latter text, Gong Yoo plays a successful businessman who, alongside countless others, contributes towards Seoul's thriving corporate system and professional identity. Clearly, he is one of many—a representative of an intense, yet successful, working space. His daughter, meanwhile, cannot communicate with a Father who is absent, both physically and emotionally. Thus, the concept and importance of the nuclear family are immediately called into question (as they also are within *The Host*). From the outset, *Train to Busan* establishes character dilemmas that are expected to be (efficiently) resolved in the face of disaster, though this is not always the case. As Jinhee Choi argues, one of the most distinguishing features of the Korean blockbuster is a 'tragic ending', in which protagonists 'only partially achieve their goals' (Choi 2010, p. 48). This is a marked difference from the typically cathartic and resolute conclusions of Hollywood cinema. In instances such as these, the protagonist is used as a secondary device, designed to filter, absorb and ultimately survive the spectacular events of the narrative (and thus satisfy the generic expectations of the audience).

In contrast, *Train to Busan* places particular emphasis on its many characters, via diegetic isolation, and endeavours to focalise them as primary narrative catalysts. For example, it is only through the interaction with other passengers on the train, most notably with an expectant Mother and Father and two elderly sisters (or 'ajummas'), that some form of affection is eventually reinstated between Gong Yoo and his child. By weaving different narratives in this way, *Train to Busan* does not rely on one singular component to drive the story, instead choosing to bring together the many facets of Korean national identity and utilise the recognisable 'roles' that have been embedded within the landscape throughout history. All the passengers, in their own unique way, encapsulate a Korean way of life, and the film uses this platform as an opportunity to explore how such characters might successfully exist alongside one another.

Elsewhere, there is also a group of high school teenagers, a homeless man and a villainous corporate executive whose 'ruthless' behaviour, as Tony Rayns observes, 'deliberately recalls recent [national] scandals involving a ferry company and Korean Air' (Rayns 2016, p. 93). Inevitably, when these characters are in a claustrophobic train carriage together—a space that functions as a purgatorial realm between two major cities— issues of class inequality and social injustice are regularly foregrounded. If Busan is a heavenly space of sanctuary and safety, Seoul is its hellish and doomed counterpart. This is suggested from the beginning of the film, as the capital city is the first to succumb to the infected. It is also worth mentioning that, not coincidentally, Seoul's destruction is attributed to it geographical position, as it is implied that the virus originates from the North (close to, or perhaps even across, the border). Thus, the closer we get to the city of Busan, which rests at the southernmost point of the Korean peninsula, the more likely we are to escape the 'threat'.

The suggestion of a specific kind of political tension is certainly present, but it only ever remains as such: a suggestion. What does remain clear, however, is the allegorical divide between the two spaces. This juxtaposition places further emphasis on the train itself and its journey across the landscape, as both are used to question the likeliness of survival for most of, if not all, the characters present. The same can be said for the river and the surrounding metropolis in *The Host*. Both texts use spaces of isolation to interrogate the functionality and purpose of their characters. Both the train carriage and the Han River equate to a subversive zone of judgement. Judgement by who exactly is left fairly ambiguous, but it is evident that the conclusive state of each character is largely dependent upon their actions and the choices they make within these symbolic environments.

As we venture further down the line in *Train in Busan* and escape becomes futile, tensions and accusations intensify between the passengers. Not only does the film establish parallel narrative development between the physical and the personal here (as each 'stage' of the attack is matched by an equal emphasis on interior character conflict), but it also uses the spatial boundaries of the train to further illuminate the threat of the 'monster', in all its forms. While the clear and present danger takes the form of the infected, *Train to Busan* simultaneously draws attention to the primitive and innate menace of human nature, an equal threat that is less likely to be contained. This is certainly a defamiliarising approach to character construction, simply because there is no immediate figure on whom one can rely to navigate the journey through the filmic world. The majority of Hollywood disaster movies rely on the 'star' protagonist to ground the events—*Independence Day* (1996), *Armageddon* (1998), *The Day After Tomorrow* (2004) and *War of the Worlds* (2005) are just a few well-known examples that closely follow this formula. The characters in *Train to Busan*, nevertheless, are not, by contrast, instantly likeable beings; they each subvert the pre-conceived image of the standard blockbuster character—a cinematic fixture that is mostly consistent, coherent and to a certain extent, sympathetic.

However, whether these flawed characters are used to directly reflect certain divisions within modern Korean society or merely function as narrative constructions is an area that remains open to interpretation (and, and such, perfectly demonstrates the film's oscillation between a nationalised discourse and popular/commercial modes). Differences in class and status inevitably heighten the discord between the passengers and, more significantly, enforce a system that prioritises the safety of the affluent and the influential. The commands of rich executive Yon-Suk, for example, are often more readily accepted than the advice offered by the homeless man, who incidentally discovers the infected first and attempts to warn the others. Gong Yoo, in an equally powerful manner, tells his daughter to only 'look out' for herself and to disregard the welfare of others. Yet, even with these conversations, it is still difficult to determine whether these disputes represent a more universal experience of contemporary social adversity, as opposed to one that is specifically Korean. Evidently, such issues are addressed, though never in a way that interferes with the efficiency, linearity and movement of the narrative (hence a return to the 'typical' blockbuster model). Just as one quarrel begins, another attack by the infected soon follows, effectively halting, but not entirely removing, any prolonged focus on social commentary and criticism. Given that the characters are clearly Korean constructions and are born from a distinctively Korean landscape, its emphasis remains despite the progression and pressure of the narrative.

For this reason, the train itself is instrumental in allowing the text to simultaneously uphold and abandon certain blockbuster tropes. It not only acts as the primary setting in which chaos can sufficiently unfold (and thus satisfy obligations of spectacle) but also operates as a symbolic time capsule that shelters and isolates a concentrated version of Korean society. A version of 'Seoul' is certainly present in each carriage, albeit on a much smaller and more intimate scale. The train is therefore responsible for reinforcing and sustaining cultural specificity as it ultimately manipulates and drastically narrows the focus of the audience. Even when the capital city is not physically present on screen, and characters are separated from it, our attention never strays from the 'idea' of it, which is of paramount importance when considering how Seoul is so often used to inform, shape and determine the South Korean national paradigm.

Setting is paramount to social symbolism. Just like the Han River in *The Host*, the main setting of *Train to Busan* conveys a relentless sense of movement and transformation. Neither a body of water nor a train carriage is ever truly stationary or static—the former develops *alongside* an evolving landscape and the latter *travels* through it. These spaces, whilst remote and solitary, are constantly changing and are therefore appropriate for the many characters who must, as blockbuster narratives would have us believe, experience some kind of emotional enhancement. Unlike the river, however, the train allows its passengers to temporarily exist outside of the 'physical' presentation of Seoul, that is to say a concrete, and to a certain extent familiar, articulation of the cityscape. The characters are certainly products of an intensely urban environment, but it is rarely assumed that they cannot exist or function outside of this space, as the film demonstrates by its conclusion. This may be regarded as an attempt to diverge from the globally conceptualised image of South Korea and momentarily abandon the perception of the country from a broad, exterior perspective. We must instead rely on the characters, their dispositions and their relationships, to build an informed portrait of the social and cultural landscape. Thus, the evocation of self-determined nationalisation is once again made evident and its ultimate goal rendered plain—to celebrate the expansive, comprehensive and resilient nature of the Korean self, wherever it is manifested.

The notion that Korean national identity is static, therefore, is once again challenged by the understanding that there is a permanent connection between South Korea's capital city and the urban self: even if the two are physically separated, they remain psychologically and emotionally attached. Seoul does not necessarily need to be on screen to be felt; it can also exist as a permeating presence (via character, historical suggestion, the evocation of urban existence, etc.). This therefore implies that while the capital city is crucial, and it functions in a specific way, it is by no means unitary or homogenous. Seoul, and all that it represents, remain polypresent at all times. Even when fully visualised on screen, there is a sense of symbolic layering embedded within every corner of modern artifice. As mentioned in the previous chapter, this perspective is emblematic of Edward Soja's 'Thirdspace', as Seoul is depicted as a peripheral, sometimes transient and occasionally transformable landscape—but a definably national South Korean landscape nonetheless.

The fact that this urban, architectural and cultural symbolism is realised within a text that can also, on a basic level, be read as a generic piece of popular cinema demonstrates the extent to which the Korean approach revitalises the former conception of the blockbuster. We often consider urban space as symptomatic of such texts, given that many use the metropolis as a complimentary backdrop to the action. Urbanity equates to modernism and the 'new', and thus is often a requirement within the blockbuster model. It is rare, however, for these spaces to carry such social, historical and cultural gravity and ultimately function as something *other* than a standard cinematic setting. Contemporary Korean cinema is not only aware of this, but it also aims to establish the city as a principal national signifier and therefore avoid the current Western pattern of urban obscurity and facelessness (in which one cinematic metropolis can be easily exchanged for another).

Postmodern Vistas: Reflections, Reproductions and the Dual Nature of Identity

In *Train to Busan*, the carnage and destruction of Seoul is often presented to us through a separate lens, whether in a news report or through a phone screen—a hyper-modern delivery of the filmic space. Similarly, the first attack sequence in *The Host* shows terrified onlookers reaching for their phones, or bus passengers observing the chaotic spectacle through a window, as though they have their own personal movie screen. Even at these early stages, both films are treating their own narratives with a degree of self-awareness by drawing attention to the hyper-modernised plight of the diegetic world, as well as the characters that exist within it, including those from a much older generation. This reference to technology, presented as a key story-telling tool, complicates narrative order and delivery. Formal elements that we would typically associate with the genre, namely those of coherency, linearity and a level of 'spectatorial distance', are continuously undermined. Despite the fantastical circumstances, we can draw parallels between the 'real' world and the 'reel' world, so that the space on screen appears slightly less inauthentic and/or constructed.

Particularly in *Train to Busan*, the depiction of various events resembles a real-time, documentary-esque news bulletin. At each stage of the train journey, we learn more of the scale and devastation caused by the 'outbreak', as though information is deliberately withheld and released to match the pacing of the narrative and the speed of the train on which we too are a passenger. Rather than place us in a position of omniscience and safety, *Train to Busan* immediately seeks to dissolve the veil of separation between diegetic and non-diegetic narration, meaning that our own experiences are largely parallel to those of the characters on screen and our knowledge equally as limited. Furthermore, the repetitive use of reflections not only diversifies the way that the monsters are presented to us (daughter Soo-Ah's gaze upon her own mirror image in the train window is abruptly interrupted by an attack), but it is also designed to illuminate the tension between the outer 'societal' performance of the characters and their inner, authentic selves. During a momentary stop at Daejeon station, a surprise attack from the infected results in a collective attempt to barricade two large glass doors. The mirroring in this scenario is blatant, as the male characters must directly face their inhuman counterparts, many of whom are (or were) soldiers, still wearing their ravaged and blood-soaked uniforms.

Evidently, the passengers do experience a sense of horror in this moment, given that they are looking at men who were once amongst the most revered and respected of Korean citizens. The country has, and continues to be, a heavily militarised state, with an unparalleled sense of duty and patriotism (as is evidenced by the mandatory military service law). Thus, the feeling of loss in this scene is especially poignant. More significant, however, is how the glass is used to articulate two antithetical, yet equally valid, forms of Korean masculine identity. Gong Yoo's character, clad in a sleek business suit, white shirt and expensive wristwatch, is forced to acknowledge the man on the 'other side' and all that he represents—a uniformed and heroic symbol of Korea's historical and national consciousness. It is also very likely that the character, on some level, recognises his younger self in the infected soldier, presumably because he too has completed his national conscription in the past. Moments such as these are used to not only address the scale of the attack but also illuminate Seoul's diverse social plains and polyphonic landscape.

Indeed, both *Train to Busan* and *The Host* endeavour to show the inherently layered nature of identity, and of South Korean identity especially, through the reflective and bountiful prisms of an intensely modern metropolis. The characters function on several different cultural, filmic and symbolic levels. There are hidden complexities penetrating these ostensibly Korean stereotypes, which are emphatically manifested by the conclusions of both films. Arguably, this reiterates a national cinematic trope. There is the sense that it is entirely necessary to acknowledge recognisable social institutions, sensibilities and landscapes, but this is gradually overshadowed by the desire to further unravel the archetypal Korean patterns born from these established backdrops and/or spaces. The characters in both texts are indicative of this because, as the narratives progress, so too does their purpose within the story-world. Ultimately, they all operate on several different levels, very similar to the city in which they live. By equating the Seoul construct to a hyper-modern, reflective and reproductive space, in which narratives are both embedded within, and produced by, other images, *Train to Busan* draws attention to a hybridised Korean identity. These ideas are, of course, revealed in a highly postmodern and self-aware manner, which has become intrinsic to contemporary

Korean film practice, but this in no way diminishes their validity and relevance—it only serves to emphasise it. The fact that this is all realised in a text that may otherwise be labelled as a 'blockbuster' draws attention to the urgency with which we must actively reevaluate our pre-conceptions of popular cinema when it is located outside of Hollywood and the American film industry.

THE DOMINATION OF THE KOREAN BLOCKBUSTER

South Korea's big-budget ventures demonstrate a relentless pattern of success, with both audiences and critics alike. The country's highest earning films, of which *Shiri*, *Train to Busan* and *The Host* are prime examples, endeavour to integrate both substance and style—they continually focalise a distinctive national narrative whilst simultaneously delivering the expected level of cinematic 'thrill'. Evidently, there is a desire to maintain national control and character within these texts, as well as a need to re-establish and reinvent conventional discourses by implementing an ever-expanding filter of South 'Korean-ness' (by openly acknowledging and celebrating Korean national identity, in all its forms). Even though our understanding of popular cinema, particularly in its infancy, is inextricably bound to an established Hollywood concept and/or image, the often explorative nature of world cinema means that it is now perceived as something far more transformative and arbitrary. This can also be applied to the international conception of the blockbuster, a textual framework that can incorporate a variety of different film styles, narratives and, most importantly, genres. As Julian Stringer appropriately summarises, Korean film in particular demonstrates how genre 'is a process to be observed, rather than a fixed destination to be arrived at', which infers a level of flexibility with regard to how popular cinematic models are read and later reimagined (Stringer 2005, p. 95). The South Korean film industry does not problematise or challenge the concrete nature of genre discourse, but rather aims to reconsider the approach towards, and integration of, its primary characteristics. As a consequence, this renders the once hegemonic process of film categorisation as a fairly redundant and futile practice (in the context of South Korean national cinema, at least).

When at the discretion of the local industry, the global paradigms of popular cinema, whilst not necessarily abandoned altogether, can appear distorted and, more significantly, altered by a specifically 'Korean' cultural or social approach. Rather than attempt to locate the ways in which Korean cinema satisfies genre, or place a specific genre *onto* a film, it is perhaps more productive to isolate the text and consider its position on a much broader stylistic spectrum. One way in which this can evidently be achieved is through the closer examination of the cinematic city and how it continues to be addressed within the country's millennial cinematic texts. The articulation of the urban space often brings to light a number of generic disturbances, as the transformative nature of Seoul (both as a construct and as an 'authentic' representation) is often mirrored by, and exists within, the narrative, style and form of the film. The contemporary growth of, and interest in, South Korean film has been largely aided by the simultaneous development of Seoul and the recognition of a now deeply modern, economically 'sound' and progressive urban society (at least when compared to the state of the country 40 or 50 years ago). As of 2022, South Korea currently sits within the top ten largest economies in the world, and it is arguably the image of Seoul (which sits at the centre of urban, economic, social and cultural policy) that acts as a primary representation of South Korea's many successes.[2] Its constructed image is synonymous with the country's positive social, cultural and global advancement, to the extent that it now exists as a portrait, or symbol, of change and triumph. South Korea remains very aware of this, often allowing its capital city to engage with the desires of an insatiable touristic gaze.

This remains a key reason why Seoul has featured so prominently in Korean films like *The Host, Train to Busan* or, more recently, *Parasite,* and why it is now acknowledged on an expansive international platform. One need to only look at the recent endeavours of Hollywood filmmaking to understand the extent to which Seoul has secured a place on the world stage. Marvel's *Black Panther* (2018) and *Avengers: Age of Ultron* (2015), for example, have both set a significant portion of their story in South Korea (one in the second largest city of Busan, the other in Seoul). The latter in particular makes it clear to the audience that Seoul is a new and distinctive setting, worthy of a significant level of exploration—and not simply on the cinema screen. The capital is not used as a 'standard' landscape that can be exchanged for any other. Instead, it is utilised as a crucial space in which to further develop the movement of the narrative. This presents a crucial and telling divergence from standard Hollywood practice, in which the regular usage of Canadian locations and production

---

[2] Silver, C. 2022. The World's Top 20 Economies. *Investopedia*. https://www.investopedia.com/insights/worlds-top-economie. Accessed 13th October 2022.

spaces succeeds only in creating and sustaining an anonymous America on screen.[3]

The dynamic and inimitable image of modern South Korea, on the other hand, satisfies a certain sense of cinematic spectacle that Hollywood and its many interchangeable urban vistas simply cannot. While this choice may have been a strategic marketing technique for the Marvel Studios (given that East Asian audiences significantly contribute to the international box office), the continuous attention on Seoul is indicative of a renewed and constantly growing global interest. This suggests that the manner in which this city is perceived and rendered, cinematically or otherwise, both nationally and internationally, is the result of a unique, shared focus. As Kim So-Young observes, South Korea has demonstrated a synchronised 'desire for cinema and desire for globalisation', which have paved the way for 'an emergence of new [Korean] identities' (Kim 2005, pp. 83–87). Furthermore, this unprecedented growth of cinephilia has rendered Seoul as a site of symbolic, cultural and historical conflation. The celluloid image of Korea has thus integrated with the present national consciousness and, in light of Kim's observation, has created a space in which to further debate the contemporary notion of the Korean self and its various complexities.

The industry's concentrated blockbuster releases have clearly succeeded in taking this national exploration further and have projected these questions of identity to a global audience in a manner that is culturally specific, yet accessible. South Korean cinema remains aware of history and has a tendency to explore the implications of such (both directly and indirectly), but these cultural enquiries are often used to educate, enlighten and reflect, not necessarily to blame or criticise—especially so in the post-millennial era. The country's complex associations with 'outsiders' help to fuel a contemporary investigation into the social, psychological and cultural discourses embedded within the modern-day Korean body (which includes both individual and collective national consciousness). Ultimately, the blockbuster greatly facilitates this motion.

While it is entirely possible to argue that there is less academic or critical gravity to be found in such a text (as opposed to a piece of art cinema, for example), Darcy Paquet observes how Korean cinema promotes a sense of

---

[3] From *Brokeback Mountain* (2005) to *Mean Girls* (2004), and from *American Psycho* (2000) to *X-Men* (2000), many contemporary, post-millennial American films are now shot in Canada, despite offering what is supposed to be a distinctive American narrative.

readerly oscillation, whereby 'one hesitates to distinguish unilaterally between art-house cinema and commercial cinema … since on closer analysis such distinctions usually rest on unstable foundations' (Paquet 2009, p. 83). The primary way that this has been achieved in Korea is through the increased focus on Seoul and the continued efforts to combine the cultural intricacies of Korean society with the grand narratives of popular cinema (and, by extension, the mythologised/cinematic gravitas of the cityscape). The blockbuster, more so than any other film category, acknowledges the inherently celluloid dynamic between construction, imagination and 'reality'—especially where urban space is concerned. While such narratives may be fantastical, otherworldly or make-believe, the worlds in which they unfold can be familiar, and characters instantly identifiable. The blockbuster is able to sensationalise the ordinary and, more importantly, place emphasis on particular issues in an accessible and lucid way. Modern South Korean cinema often employs this double narrative, regularly using the capital city as a broad canvas on which to paint the spectacular and the symbolic in equal measure. Collectively, this again reinforces an expansive, yet uniquely Korean film movement—the Seoul genre.

Conclusion

It is perfectly acceptable to read the vast array of characters in *Train to Busan* and *The Host* as outwardly generic and standardised 'blockbuster' figures, or even view Seoul as a functional landscape designed to serve a paradigmatic purpose. To a certain extent, the films want the spectator to engage with their narratives in this recognisable way, as to read or approach such texts in this manner attests to their global accessibility, cinematic appeal and generally engaging discourse. Indeed, both texts clearly satisfy the common obligations of spectacle and, in relation to Julian Stringer's observation, the aforementioned notion of 'size', which remains structurally paramount to the production and exhibition of popular, commercial filmmaking. Thus, in their most rudimentary state, these films will always operate as examples of pure, unequivocal entertainment, which again problematises the perceived *functional* differences between the American and the South Korean blockbuster text.

However, I would suggest this reading significantly alters when considering various contextual factors, such as the industry in which these films have been produced and the audiences for whom they are ultimately intended. The capacity to convey meaning within any text is almost entirely at the discretion of the reader: their choices, approaches and, above all else, the intensity of their personal engagement. For a Korean audience, therefore, *The Host* and *Train to Busan* operate far beyond their emphatic blockbuster appearance and ostensibly conventional style. Questions of national identity are regularly addressed here, and they are presented within distinguishable Korean landscapes, projected through culturally distinctive narratives and voiced by characters who are intrinsically linked to the metropolis in which they exist. This is not to say that such texts are impenetrable from a global perspective, as previously noted, nor does it suggest that national specificity is lost on the international spectator. It merely demonstrates how these films seek to portray the intricacies of national character in a manner that positively differentiates the Korean film industry from other world cinemas, their filmmakers and collective cultural objectives. Therefore, a fundamental sense of separateness, not necessarily opposition, must be established between the (Hollywood) blockbuster and the South Korean conception and manifestation of such. Only then can we begin to unlock the potential mutations that remain buried in this seemingly generic formula and, more importantly, prevent Hollywood from maintaining its long-established position as 'the referential point to which or against which the idea of national cinema is mobilised', as Ok Hye-Ryoung notes (Ok 2009).

Ultimately, the South Korean film industry has recognised the blockbuster's capacity for change, renewal and national reconfiguration. As a result, the genre's former allegiance to Hollywood has been interrogated and its previously Americanised model put under an intense level of scrutiny. Thus, the present 'ownership' of the blockbuster and its future 'place' within the wider, global film community remain undetermined. This should not, however, be perceived as a negative outcome, but rather an opportunity to question and reposition the impact, role and situation of commercial cinema in its entirety. This is what South Korean cinema has sought to achieve throughout the past 20 years, during its crucial 'new wave' period and, latterly, in its renaissance age; to re-conceptualise the blockbuster by implanting unique, national inflections within its malleable template. To date, this has proved to be a greatly successful endeavour.

REFERENCES

Choi, J. 2010. *The South Korean Film Renaissance*, 2010. Middletown, Connecticut: Wesleyan University Press.
Cucco, M. 2009. The Promise is Great: The Blockbuster and the Hollywood Economy. *Media, Culture and Society* 31 (2): 215–230. https://doi.org/10.1177/0163443708100315.
Diffrient, D.S. 2003. South Korean Film Genres and Art-House Anti-Poetics: Erasure and Negation in the Power of Kangwan Province. *Cineaction* 60: 60–71.
Kim, S. 2005. Cine-Mania' or Cinephilia: Film Festivals and The Identity Question. In *New Korean Cinema*, ed. Julian Stringer and Chi-Yun Shin, 79–92. Edinburgh: Edinburgh University Press.
Klein, C. 2008. Why American Studies Needs to Think About Korean Cinema, or, Transnational Genres in the Films of Bong Joon Ho. *American Quarterly* 60 (4): 871–898. https://doi.org/10.1353/aq.0.0041.
Lee, N., and J.Y. 2011. Localized Globalization and a Monster National: 'The Host' and the South Korean Film Industry. *Cinema Journal* 50 (3): 45–61. https://doi.org/10.1353/cj.2011.0031.
Levin, N.D., and Y. Han. 2002. *Sunshine in Korea: The South Korean Debate Over Policies Toward North Korea*. Santa Monica, CA: RAND.
Maltby, R. 2003. *Hollywood Cinema*. 2nd ed. Oxford: Blackwell.
Ok, H. 2009. The Politics of The Korean Blockbuster: Narrating the Nation and the Spectacle of 'Glocalisation' in '2009 Lost Memories'. *The Spectator, Los Angeles* 29 (2): 37–46.
Paquet, D. 2009. *New Korean Cinema; Breaking the Waves*. New York: Columbia University Press.
Park, S. 2007. Korean Cinema after Liberation: Production, Industry, and Regulatory Trends. In *Seoul Searching: Culture and Identity in Contemporary Korean Cinema*, ed. Frances Gateward, 15–36. Albany: State University of New York Press.
Rayns, T. 2016. Train to Busan—Review. *Sight and Sound* 26: 93.
Ryoo, W. 2009. Globalization, or the Logic of Cultural Hybridization: The Case of the Korean Wave. *Asian Journal of Communication* 19 (2): 137–151. https://doi.org/10.1080/01292980902826427.
Silver, C. 2022. The World's Top 20 Economies. *Investopedia*. Accessed 13 October 2022. https://www.investopedia.com/insights/worlds-top-economie.
Stringer, J. 2003. *Movie Blockbusters*. London: Routledge.
———. 2005. Putting Korean Cinema in its Place: Genre Classifications and The Contexts of Reception. In *New Korean Cinema*, ed. Julian Stringer and Chi-Yun Shin, 95–105. Edinburgh: Edinburgh University Press.
———. 2010. Storming the Big Screen: The Shiri Syndrome. In *Seoul Searching: Culture and Identity in Contemporary Korean Cinema*, ed. Frances Gateward, 55–72. Albany: State University of New York Press.

CHAPTER 4

The Hyper-masculine City

Masculinity and the focalisation of the complex male figure have always been key interrogative tropes within South Korean cinema. Throughout its turbulent history, the South Korean film industry has endeavoured to explore the ambivalent relationship between masculinity and a broader sense of national identity. Despite having concrete and distinctive phases of growth and development, one feature that has continuously connected, and perhaps united, the various cinematic movements in South Korean film is a persistent focus on the social, political and ideological evolution of masculinity. However, the intensity of this focus is indicative of a culturally and nationally specific concern, and therefore has a greater, and significantly more complex, purpose. The presentation of Korean masculinity, in all its filmic forms, is symptomatic of the perceived advancement and social evolution of the country as a whole, which suggests that the overarching thematic concerns in Korean cinema have shifted alongside a changing patriarchal landscape. While this is, to a certain extent, problematic (as other Korean identities have been marginalised by the persistent privileging of the male experience on screen), it demonstrates the determination with which the industry has perpetuated the links between masculinity and nationhood. Furthermore, it has used this focus to subsequently distance itself even further from other East Asian cinemas.

© The Author(s), under exclusive license to Springer Nature Switzerland AG 2023
G. Ballard, *Urban Landscapes and National Visions in Post-Millennial South Korean Cinema*, East Asian Popular Culture, https://doi.org/10.1007/978-3-031-29739-7_4

Kelly Jeong suggests that given South Korea's 'strong tradition of patriarchy', it is entirely possible that the 'state perceives the nation as a collective, universally male subject'—a result of its previous relations with Japanese Imperialism, controversial governments and/or dictatorships, the influence of authoritarian figures and the continued enforcement of martial law (Jeong 2006, p. 129). This creates a paradoxical cycle, whereby the 'tradition of patriarchy' that Jeong refers to is largely a consequence of, and simultaneously a contributor towards, the systemic periods of violence and trauma that occurred across the Korean landscape throughout the Twentieth century. Thus, Korean masculinity has long remained deeply intertwined with the military and, more importantly, narratives of conflict, duty, national honour and war. The current mandatory service law (which now involves conscription for all Korean men between the ages of 18 and 35) is further evidence of this continuing tradition.

These collective attitudes towards a 'masculine nation' have also been informed, and perhaps magnified, by South Korea's historic engagement with aspects of a dominantly Confucian culture (alongside the continued recognition of its most fundamental practices and values, especially concerning family structure and societal roles). The ideological interdependence between Confucianism and an uncompromising masculine hegemony has significantly influenced the condition of Korean society in the past and, indeed, the present. The preservation of the domestic household is paramount to Confucian thought and with it, the acceptance of familial hierarchy and a 'male-oriented' social order. Therefore, (Korean) Confucianism may be characterised, as So-Yi Chung maintains, as the 'cradle of rigidity and coercion' (Chung 2016, p. 631). Fundamentally, the overriding Confucian mindset preserves a structure that supports a dominant masculinity and further privileges the patriarchal systems in which these 'hyper-male' identities exist—particularly where family relationships are concerned.

However, this does not necessarily mean that all Confucian values are to be rejected or replaced by more liberal and modern sensibilities. While there is now a growing and substantial level of resistance forming against certain aspects of these historic philosophies, orders and ideologies (mainly with regard to issues of equality in the workplace and social morality), the impact of traditional Confucianism and its subsequent limitations to gender roles are still evident within most forms of popular Korean culture (Jin 2016). This is largely because it has provided a solid foundation on which to build national identity, social discipline and a balanced Korean consciousness. As Yi Myonggu and William Douglas observed in their readings of the post-liberation space of South Korea, 'Family relationships, political attitudes, approaches to problem-solving and many other aspects of Korean life show the imprint of the Confucian tradition', despite its 'state influence' ending in the early Twentieth century (Myonggu and Douglas 1967, p. 43).

To a certain extent, these values remain important to the formation and continuation of a congruent and historically aware Korean society. Nevertheless, the narratives that have manifested from these practices are problematic, particularly when concerning the aforementioned evolution of South Korean 'maleness'. Since its transposition from the beliefs of a largely patriarchal Korean society into an equally patriarchal Korean culture, masculine identity has stood at the political, social and cultural centre of the complex Confucian paradigm and, latterly, a narrowly gendered discourse. When placed alongside the concept of 'nationhood', Korean masculinity has been centralised within the social consciousness in a way that female identity never has. To illuminate further this gendered bias, one must inevitably look to some of the defining moments in South Korea's history, particularly the events that shaped the development of cultural production, both in industry and practice, and, by extension, the perceived characteristics of Korean national identity in popular entertainment.

TROUBLED BEGINNINGS: QUESTIONING POST-WAR MASCULINITY

During the Twentieth century, not only did the Japanese occupation (formally 1910–1945) severely impede the social and cultural progress of South Korea, the following war against North Korea and its allies significantly altered the national landscape and forever changed the lives of those who survived it. Many Korean films made in the subsequent decade, between 1955 and 1970, known as the 'Golden Age', sought to articulate the post-war plight of the soldiers that were directly involved and thus address the long-established, historically prevalent concept of 'soldierly masculinity' (Tikhonov 2007). Conflicting concepts of 'manhood', domestic place and 'male belonging' were the main interests of these narratives because, as Kelly Jeong continues, 'a threat to the nationhood of Korea can also, by extension, be interpreted as a threat to the Korean masculine subject', and vice versa (Jeong 2006, p. 129). Director Yu Hyun Mok's classic *Obaltan* (1961), or *The Stray/Aimless Bullet* as it is alternatively known, is a text that focuses on these anxieties by emphasising an intensely dark, hopeless and melancholy post-war landscape. The film follows an array of different characters as they attempt to cope and acclimatise in a drastically changed post-war Korea. However, while all (including female characters) are clearly victims of this distinctive setting, it is the male characters (of which there are many) who remain the primary focus. A sense of inter-generational male despair pervades the narrative, which is used to challenge, though not necessarily diminish, the supposed ideals of Confucian masculinity.

There are numerous and deliberate conversations that take place between the male characters, many of which address the war and its effect on the collective masculine psyche. During these private, all-male interactions, which often take place in bars over copious amounts of alcohol, we are made aware that the army is, to a large extent, a place that reaffirms ideas of the self. It facilitates a 'space' or 'community' that instils purpose, social function and, most importantly, 'spirit', as the character Yeongho proclaims, who despairs at his inability to find employment after leaving the army. Meanwhile, as the men ponder their own social existence, or lack thereof, it is implied that Korean women are offering sexual services to American soldiers in the surrounding urban streets of Seoul. In this instance, the presence of the West poses a direct threat to the formation of post-war masculinity in Korea. There is a sense of oppositional masculinities in conflict with one another here and ultimately, it is the Western image of maleness that overwhelms the Korean counterpart. While the Americans remain in uniform and are still technically serving a cause (however unwarranted their presence may be), the Korean men are left without any military recognition, reward or identity.

Therefore, the growing level of national anxiety, and particularly male anxiety, is quickly made apparent, as is the increasing, collective disappointment in a political system that has grown desensitised to the predicament of the Korean people in the post-war climate. It is worth noting here that, ordinarily, such strong social and political criticism during the 'Golden Age' of Korean cinema would have been promptly abridged by the state. *Obaltan*, nevertheless, was released during a brief, yet fortuitous, transitional period: after the conclusion of Rhee Syngman's presidency (1960) and before the instatement of Park Chung Hee's regime (1963). As a consequence, government censorship and the rules regarding what could, and could not, be shown on film, were temporarily weakened. Therefore, *Obaltan*, perhaps even more so than any other film of the time, was able to communicate the concerns of a post-war society in a manner that was authentic, honest and intrinsically *Korean* because it was not stifled by the former levels of regulatory, governmental intrusion. It remains a pivotal anti-establishment text—deliberately confrontational and accusatory in nature.

Nevertheless, while *Obaltan* remains successful in its portrayal of the impoverished landscape of post-war Korea and clearly recognises the scale of human tragedy the political landscape manifests, this vision is once again filtered predominantly via the male gaze and/or experience. This is most notably and symbolically realised through the main protagonist Cheolho's persistent toothache, for which he refuses to seek any medical assistance. Even though the cause of his resistance is left fairly ambiguous, one might argue that it is linked to the concept of pain, both physically and emotionally. Ultimately, Cheolho must identify, endure and accept his own pain. He has to feel something, something against which he can direct his own despair, which paradoxically can confirm his 'aimless' existence. Indeed, this desire to rediscover one's own identity (as a result of loss or through the recognition of bodily pain and/or violence) has remained a key paradigm of the Korean male protagonist, from past to present. We can also expand this to the Korean nation as a whole, which for many years has been defined and characterised by a visceral sense of historical pain and trauma. Indeed, it is this pain in question that continues to be used, referenced and immortalised within Korean national consciousness—a fixed *idea* that purports to both acknowledge and, in some cases, consolidate South Korean society's complex attitudes towards the past.

Obaltan, however, demonstrates the futility of this endeavour—particularly in response to male trauma. By the concluding moments of the film, when Cheolho finally decides to have his tooth removed, there is a palpable sense of hopelessness. As he sits bleeding in a taxi, the delirious Cheolho announces that he has 'tried hard to be a good son, a good husband, a good father, a good brother', which is indicative, as Aaron Park maintains, of his desired position as 'a paragon of Confucian virtue' (Park and Joon 2017, p. 90). As arguably the most righteous and dutiful character in the film, this utterance functions as a final and emphatic reminder of masculine fragility and, rather controversially, the inherently flawed and antiquated systems perpetuated by Korean Confucianism. As Cheolho's mind and body are, by this point, beyond repair, so too is his desire to fulfil or at least occupy the role that Korean society has bestowed upon him. His physical and mental deterioration are synonymous, and he has essentially transformed into the 'aimless bullet'—bereft of direction or purpose. There are no clear solutions here. If there are, the film refuses to divulge them, neither to the suffering characters nor the spectator. Only an abundance of questions and a general sense of disquietude remain, concerning not only the fate of Cheolho but also perhaps, the fate of South Korea itself.

Throughout this pivotal era of early Korean cinema, of which *Obaltan* is undoubtedly a prime example, the desire to locate a coherent and consistent kind of masculinity is evident. *Obaltan* draws attention to this desire through its persistent focus on the aforementioned army experience and its supposed ability to forge a bond between the Korean male subject and national identity. More importantly, the film, alongside similar historical Korean texts such as *The Coachman* (1961), *Romance Papa* (1960) and *A Tender Heart* (1967), demonstrates a collective need to *place* the male figure within a zone of rationality, reliability and strength. *Obaltan* remains a text that not only highlights the difficulties of achieving this but also questions whether it is an idea that should be pursued at all, particularly as a response to either the apprehensions raised by national trauma or as an acknowledgement of the expectations created within a post-war society. The film remains highly aware of itself through its negotiation of several character perspectives, acutely navigating the conversations of war, conflict and the military in a manner that never fully supports or rejects the opinions of its main male characters. Fundamentally, *Obaltan* is ambivalent and confrontational in equal measure.

Nevertheless, the film still acknowledges the importance of sustaining these conversations, even if it seems impossible to draw resolute conclusions. Since this successful 'Golden' period of Korean cinema, the desire to seek answers has never faded, nor has the exploration of the ambivalent 'Korean man' dwindled. *Obaltan* was one of only a few texts that initiated this national cinematic trend, predominantly due to the temporary absence of national film regulations. This is not to say, of course, that the films which did face significant censorship guidelines were less successful in communicating critical ideas. Despite the prolonged periods in which government restrictions compromised narrative authenticity and creative freedom, the Korean film industry has continuously strived to articulate the voices and anxieties of the society for whom its productions are ultimately intended, albeit through an intensely masculine filter. In a single generation, the Korean public 'have made the painful transition from one extreme to another'; thus, as Anthony Leong states, it is 'not surprising ... that social and political traumas are played out on the nation's movie screens' (Leong 2004, p. 185). Notably, Korean masculinity lies at the centre of the 'trauma' to which Leong refers. The concept of 'trauma' (both physical and mental), when investigated on the Korean cinema screen, is inextricably bound to the male narrative and journey. Furthermore, there is the continued sense that national memory (in which trauma can frequently be identified) remains conditioned by a masculinised historical landscape. Thus, as Korean popular culture continues to address these histories, it is important that the Korean film industry remains aware of and draws attention to a gendered past, however problematic, within its post-millennial cinematic endeavours and ostensibly modern productions.

THE NEXT PHASE: KOREAN GANGSTER FILM AND THE ULTIMATE 'ANTI-HERO'

As previously stated by Kelly Jeong, it appears that the image of the Korean nation is inextricably bound to the concept of masculinity and to the authoritative male figure. It is inevitable, therefore, that Korean popular culture should continue to address this dominant and singular presence, especially within film. Since its cinematic infancy, the pursuit of a greater understanding of masculine identity and the enigma of modern patriarchy has not altered or weakened. The only component that has changed, however, is how such issues have been articulated and presented to the evolving and, more importantly, *globalised* Korean film audience. The question of masculinity persists, but its manifestation has been reconditioned over time. Social apprehensions do not diminish; they merely morph into something greater and more specific, depending on the current social, political and cultural landscape. Thus, alongside each cinematic development, from the decline of the 1970s to the boom of the 1990s, there has also been a concurrent shift in the role, disposition and narrative function of the male protagonist.

It is also worth noting here that these various developments have been significantly influenced by the external challenges faced by the Korean film industry itself. The continued threats of censorship, economic decline, political ideology and conflict (with regard to corrupt governmental leadership) have compromised the creativity, authenticity and even the very infrastructure of the industry. It is therefore arguable that Korean national cinema, both as a practice and as an institution, has had to contend with more obstacles than most (which again substantiates the argument that it should be considered or read on an isolated, national level). The representation of masculinity remains a product of this ever-changing trajectory. Since the 1990s, the aforementioned challenges have greatly subsided, and as a result, the portrayal of the 'leading man' in Korean cinema has inevitably altered, as a reflection of both an advancing industry and the increasingly contemporary landscape in which it exists. Consequently, Korean national cinema in its present state is experiencing a period of notable success, both domestically and internationally.

This is not to say, however, that the traumas of the past can no longer be discerned on screen, nor appreciated by an increasingly globalised audience. On the contrary, the renewed focus on Korean cinema and the thriving industry in which its creations are nurtured means that narratives of the past (which refers to specific historical events) can be illuminated in an altogether more dramatic and spectacular way. Inevitably, it might be argued here that the industry is commercialising national trauma, so that history, with its many narrative intricacies, becomes a precious, bankable commodity. However, the manner in which these stories evolve and are presented to us on screen suggests that Korean cinema is continually driven by its singular, national, cultural and political agenda. Essentially, it always has a message or an overarching thematic concern, even within those texts that, initially, appear the most generic and familiar.

This is most evident in a film category that, from the late 1990s, has grown exceedingly popular with South Korean audiences. The most recent incarnation of the post-millennial 'male cinematic image' has arrived via the popular and ultra-violent gangster film, a now quintessential genre of Korean national cinema and a well-recognised staple of the problematic 'East Asian' paradigm (which is a term used in a collective and generalised manner and therefore diminishes cultural specificity). However, before it became successful in Korea, the gangster film had already enjoyed years of notable critical and commercial recognition in Hong Kong and Japan, the latter of which initiated its own 'Yakuza' genre in the late 1950s. Therefore, it would be entirely reductive to consider the Korean film industry's treatment of the gangster film in complete isolation of these previous texts, both narratively and stylistically. Each interpretation of the gangster film has, in some way, been subjected to influences far beyond the parameters of the nation in which it has been reimagined and redefined.

As a consequence, the question of cinematic ownership, when applied to this particular genre, is not always the easiest to answer, largely due to our own growing awareness, as a film audience, of different world cinemas, overlapping film categories and highly intertextual narratives. This means that the basics of film practice, of narrative and of genre have to be re-established. There are a number of fundamental signifiers that one expects to locate within the 'gangster' archetype, many of which have also undoubtedly been shaped by classical Hollywood discourse. The cinematic gangster remains a vengeful figure with a questionable moral code and is often presented to us in a dangerous, yet romanticised, way. He is a loner that has minimal contact with, or affection for, any other character (but still possesses the ability to change or 'grow'). Most importantly, however, this staple of violent cinema must be simultaneously strengthened and burdened by his own inimitable sense of power. As such, gangsters remain 'symbols of freedom and self-expression, but with a concurrent inability to control their impulses', as George Walsh observes (Walsh 2018, p. 19). The image of the gangster serves a dual function—he represents both danger and deterrent, recklessness and caution. In light of Walsh's observation, it is easy to see why the gangster figure has been popularised in South Korean cinema from the post-millennial period onwards—a time that has seen a dramatic increase in national power and soft influence. Alongside these developments, however, there have also been questions and concerns regarding *how* such power is used and exhibited (all of which can be perfectly situated within, or internalised by, the long-established and representative figure of the gangster).

To a certain extent, the Korean interpretation of the gangster genre follows many of the aforementioned 'Western' tropes (as, indeed, do the versions created by most East Asian cinemas). There are, however, a few key differences. Violence is presented in a considerably more visceral, diverse and extreme way, especially from the 1990s onwards (which may be partly due to the introduction of significantly more lenient film regulations). A violent interaction is also fully integrated within the narrative—an event around which all other stories and characters typically gather. The concept of change is imperative to the action sequence. There is a sense of palpable difference between the disposition and condition of the gangster *before* entering a fight and the man he ultimately transforms into by its conclusion. Physical altercations between characters do not act as mere instruments of spectacle; they are often used to mark a critical turning point in the story and convey certain information to the audience. More importantly, there is a specific focus, in Korean cinema more generally, on violence and its impact on, or relationship with, the 'male body' (which also explains the relevance of Cheolho's toothache in *Obaltan*). Se Young Kim maintains that 'the physical violence of the [Korean] body is key', because it exists as both 'a vehicle to represent an identity' and 'a marker of cinema, of nation, of class, of gender, of movement' (Kim 2018, pp. 510–512). This suggests that the 'male body' functions as a site in which cultural, social, political and historical narratives are contained and later 'unlocked' by the story (or, in this case, a violent episode).

Therefore, an entirely new psycho-cinematic reading is required when trying to understand the cultural significance of the Korean gangster film and its ostensibly 'generic' qualities—including the function of the standard action sequence. In the Korean incarnation of the genre, there is a parallel correlation between specific events in the narrative, historical relevancy, the presentation of the 'body' and the emotional movement of the gangster figure. Essentially, the fascination with, and fetishisation of, the 'male body' and its relationship with violence and/or pain is used to articulate years of collective male trauma and a plethora of unique social narratives. The Korean gangster thus functions as a perpetually troubled character, as he remains burdened by his connection to national (masculine) consciousness, the concept of shared crisis and a developing Korean cognizance. This may also be a result of the expectations created (whether knowingly or otherwise) by a domestic film audience, particularly amongst those who have experienced the pivotal shifts of Korean society over the past 50 years. In order for the genre to sustain its own aesthetic and thematic autonomy, it must engage with, and reflect, these national expectations. Arguably, the continued exploration of the 'male body' is a primary way of achieving this, as it satisfies both the stylistic and symbolic conventions of the genre.

The extreme presentation of violence and its visceral imprint on the body is not necessarily used simply as a device to increase spectacle. Nor does it function merely as a means of satisfying the tropes of an 'action-oriented' genre. Instead, it emphasises a narrative of punishment, pain and subsequent salvation—characteristics of Korea's own traumatic history. More importantly, violence solidifies modern Korean masculine identity, a discourse that the industry has pursued since its infancy. When violence is taken away, male identity is left exposed, vulnerable and open to certain challenges (which also relates back to *Obaltan* and the male characters' shared desire to return to the army). Therefore, conflict, or the acknowledgement of it, has become a pre-requisite for understanding and exploring 'maleness' on the Korean cinema screen, especially so within the gangster genre (which has been characterised historically in terms of its violent, exhibitionist style). Even though the delivery may appear highly contemporary, national history, identity and the acknowledgement of the past remain key components within the Korean gangster narrative. By demonstrating an awareness and appreciation for these specific cultural paradigms, the Korean film industry is able to embed national meaning into what may otherwise be a simple genre text.

Thus, the Korean gangster figure remains inextricably bound to the events of the past and the movement of his country/nation, as well as the places in which these histories materialised. He is both current and, in some ways, antiquated—a superficially modern figure that is simultaneously conditioned by the passage of time and a bygone era. This particular image is also evocative of South Korea's capital city, which functions in a similar way, both off and on the cinema screen. Setting is paramount to this genre (as it is for all Korean film). At the aesthetic, formal and thematic centre of the Korean gangster film is an unequalled engagement with the cityscape—specifically, Seoul. Similar to the characters addressed in the previous chapters of this thesis, the Korean gangster figure is also a product of a nationalised urban environment. Essentially, Seoul provides both the geographical, social and perhaps even psychological parameters in which the aforementioned 'body' can exist. There is an interdependency between the Korean gangster and the cinematic metropolis—his role within the narrative is controlled by the way in which he travels through, and communicates with, the city and those who live there. This is especially relevant now, given the increasing modernity of Seoul and the contemporary nature of the Korean gangster film.

Lately, however, there has also been a rise in Korean gangster films taking place *outside* of Seoul, in other prominent national cities such as Busan and Daegu, perhaps in an effort to diversify the cinematic landscape and widen cultural engagement. Indeed, given that these urban spaces enjoy a degree of separation from the often commercialised and overly centralised Seoul, they lend themselves well to the aesthetics of the gangster genre (which on many occasions has positioned itself within the liminal space *between* popular and art-house cinema). That being said, it seems that the increasingly hybridised representation of Seoul still provides a cinematic space in which to explore the often transgressive properties of Korean gangster narratives. Indeed, there is an interdependent dialogue occurring here. While Seoul may provide the space and scope in which to neatly situate the Korean gangster text, the genre in turn is able to defamiliarise the touristic portrait of the capital city and 'recode' the landscape (thereby providing a much more sensory experience of the urban environment).

However, one must also acknowledge the extent to which Hollywood has explored this kind of engagement in the past, particularly with East coast cities. For a director such as Martin Scorsese, a gritty and inelegant New York is imperative to the formation of the mafia/gangster landscape, as is a heavily postmodern Chicago or Miami in the crime films of Michael Mann. On film, these American cities act as highly mappable, familiar and, occasionally, generic spaces, designed to work alongside a genre that, to a certain extent, is only capable of communicating a singular, efficient and causal narrative. An element of simplicity and thematic transparency is intrinsic to these aggrandised masculine stories and, more importantly, to the mythologised figures (and cities) they celebrate. Therefore, the American version of the gangster film often functions in one way—to reaffirm and solidify the power of the cinematic anti-hero and sustain the spectacularised myth of the urban experience in the West.

Nevertheless, with regard to the cinematic presentation of Seoul and its criminal landscape there is no such myth. Even though they are both burdened by history, the Korean gangster genre and the gangster himself are by-products of a specific period in time—the 1990s onwards. Newness and [post]modernity form the outer-most layers of these representations, whilst also protecting a deeply historic centre. More significantly, the Korean gangster reflects a certain phase (or desired image) of Korean male identity: hyper-masculine, powerful, purposeful and, in some ways, liberal. This is drastically different to depictions of Korean maleness on screen earlier in the Twentieth century, in which masculinity was often thwarted or rendered impotent by a largely self-created, patriarchal anxiety (as evidenced in *Obaltan*). While such anxieties are still apparent in the gangster text, as they are in all the male-centric narratives of Korean cinema, their origins and the way in which the characters subsequently respond to them are considerably different. Fundamentally, the Korean gangster genre is the result of a rapidly modernising (and, to some extent, globalising) film industry and must bring into its operation a clear awareness of contemporary society, masculinity and urban identity. Seoul is, therefore, imperative to this construction, more so than ever before. While simultaneously evoking narratives of the past, the Korean gangster is only compatible with the Seoul of today because he reflects and represents the cultural and economic advancements of the city and the country in which it resides.

The genre has had a pivotal role in the industry's transition to the Twenty-first century (as is evidenced by the high number of successful Korean gangster films released from 2000 to 2005).[1] As previously mentioned, there has clearly been a sustained appetite for this kind of story in recent years. The main reason for this may still be linked to questions surrounding 'maleness' on screen. Ultimately, the genre reconsiders the fundamentals of cinematic masculinity and its place within contemporary society. No other national cinema does this in quite the same exaggerated way, mainly because it uses the typically male-driven narrative of the gangster film to challenge the ideology, function and, indeed, purpose of cultivating a specific kind of masculine identity. Genre in the context of Hollywood or other world cinemas cannot always be transferred easily into South Korean cinema. It is fluid and prone to mutation, which means we must not only reevaluate the supposed characteristics of certain generic forms and their functions within cinema, but we must also reconsider the once standardised approach to these forms. In this particular instance, the qualitative measures that once determined the stylistic fabric of the gangster genre are rendered incomplete and, more significantly, incongruous with the visions of a nationalised industry—an industry that clearly intends to 'bend' or manipulate the rules inaugurated by Hollywood discourse. This does not mean that Korean cinema completely abandons the innate hyper-masculinity or male-oriented landscapes that audiences have come to anticipate from the gangster narrative. It instead suggests that such displays of masculinised spectacle are linked to deeper questions and concerns about Korean patriarchy and the perceived expectations of the national male subject.

Kyung Hyun Kim, in his now seminal study, attributes this to a critical level of 'remasculinization' throughout South Korean cinema from the late 1990s, in which 'screen males' gradually emerged as 'objects of desire', designed to reflect and reaffirm a post-authoritarian state of self (Kim 2004, p. 10). This meant that, alongside the film industry itself, the concept of Korean masculinity was to undergo a process of positive change and revitalisation. Cinema was the tool with which this process could be most efficiently realised and later projected to the public, particularly

---

[1] Films such as *A Bitter Sweet Life* (2005), *Friend* (2001), *My Wife is a Gangster* (2001) and *Die Bad* (2000), amongst many others.

during the economic 'boom' of the 1990s and as a consequence of the subsequent investment in the Korean national film industry. Therefore, the 'remasculinized' presentation of the Korean male protagonist coincides with the growth of the Korean blockbuster and the industry's quest to introduce a dominant, fetishised and engaging figure endowed with agency and, as previously stated, purpose (a substantial shift from the often alienated, oppressed and helpless cinematic figures of the latter half of the Twentieth century, which was, notably, a time of decline for the film industry). This is not to say that these 'new' characters appear as flawless individuals or lack complexity and vulnerability. Rather, they possess a different kind of power and dimensionality, which is not only a reflection of the growth of the industry but also the physical, psychological and social liberation of post-millennial South Korea. Similar to the recent growth of the Korean blockbuster, the emergence and ensuing popularity of the gangster genre is also acutely symptomatic of the changing economic landscape of South Korea. The spectacular and hyper-modern presentation of the male characters within these texts coincides with a highly specific image of affluence, new capitalism and cinematic prosperity.

While it is entirely possible to argue that these recent representations evoke Westernised 'leading man' imagery, one must always take into account the filmic timeline of the Korean male protagonist in his absolute entirety. I would argue that it is now more important than ever to consider South Korean cinema from an inter-historical or trans-historical perspective in order to identify and appreciate the *reactionary* properties of contemporary Korean films (as well as observe how they incorporate direct parallels to earlier examples of Korean cinematic texts and movements). In this particular instance, it is evident that the contemporary construction of the gangster acts as a current response to years of former social, historical and political unrest—as well as the next step in the path towards 'remasculinization'. This does not necessarily infer that every modern male character follows this pattern, nor does it imply that they all serve the same function. It only demonstrates that when read on a broader cinematic spectrum, these characters often demand the same socio-cinematic interpretation that has so readily been afforded to their on-screen predecessors. To a certain extent, many examples of ostensibly accessible or 'familiar' post-millennial male characters, from the imprisoned Oh Dae-Su of *Oldboy* (2003) to the ruthless Kim Sun-Woo of *A Bittersweet Life* (2003), embody all the masculine trauma of the past 50 years within Korea.

The anxieties still exist within these figures, yet they are established in a manner that is altogether more violent, idiosyncratic and unpredictable. They remain complex beings and function far beyond the structural parameters of the genre in which they are conceived. Yet again, this breakdown of representational norms, via subversive characterisation, invites further questions about genre cinema (in the classical context) and its place within Korean filmmaking—whether it is useful, relevant or, indeed, a method with which we should 'read' or interpret a national cinema. For the gangster text this subversive approach is especially significant, as it highlights the cinematic diversity inherent within the 'male figure', and draws attention to his evolving state within certain generic frameworks. Thus, the gangster genre and all its familiar signifiers inherit entirely different meanings when considered in a purely *Korean* context.

As a result, one must reconsider the generalisation and supposed transferability of genre. When the gangster paradigm functions on a singularly Korean level, it illuminates a culturally specific discourse—one that cannot be easily exchanged with that of any other national cinema. Consequently, this provides the Korean film industry (alongside its key directors, themes, characters and stories) with a level of cinematic autonomy and creative independence, which may explain the popularity of the gangster genre in Korea. What was once an American construction, drenched in Western myth, is now a text that can be understood and read in terms of its 'Koreanised' symbolism. More importantly, Korean cinema's unique treatment of the genre means that it is not only possible, but necessary, to sustain a degree of separateness between its own version of gangster cinema, the crime films of Hong Kong and, more significantly, Japan's cinematic Yakuza tradition (which, for some time, has acted as the stylistic 'benchmark' against which all other gangster texts are measured). While some filmic superimposition may still exist between these cinematic movements, each textual variation can, and should, be read independently, primarily because each industry represents different values, histories, ideas and cultural attitudes.

Fragile Figures: Identity and Place in *The Man from Nowhere*

The modern and socially ostracised outlaw (played by Won Bin) in Lee Jeong Beom's *The Man from Nowhere* (2010) is a prime example of the ongoing exploration of cinematic masculinity and its relationship with the gangster genre (and the idiosyncrasies of such when explored in Korean film). To understand how and why the film so emphatically addresses this complex connection, we must once again return to a 'golden age' predecessor. While it initially appears as though *The Man from Nowhere* shares little in common with classic texts like *Obaltan* (with regard to story, time and place), the themes of manhood, nation and identity still persist and are perhaps magnified by an overtly modernised setting and stylised aesthetic. Similarly to *Obaltan*, *The Man from Nowhere* also re-introduces the ubiquitous notion of 'soldierly masculinity', as it is eventually made plain, through separate conversations, that the main character, Tae Sik, has a violent, military past (which, evidently, he uses to his advantage as the narrative progresses) (Tikhonov 2007). Thus, despite the significant stylistic distance between *Obaltan* and *The Man from Nowhere*, it is clear that thematic patterns from the former continually re-emerge in the latter. This again demonstrates why it is now necessary to take a trans-historical approach to such texts (given that there is evidence of narrative interdependency) and why modern South Korean cinema should be considered as inherently *reactionary* in nature.

Tae-Sik is a character who lives outside of the established social system and/or order, yet is still entirely dependent upon, and embedded within, the Korean landscape. He is, therefore, a social and filmic contradiction—physically bound to a place with which he shares no emotional, or even physical, attachment. His appearance and demeanour often juxtapose his surroundings, which suggests that he occupies a space entirely detached from the present reality of the film. Often depicted as a dark, suited figure, the enigmatic Tae-Sik does little to represent the impoverished urban community in which he resides. On the one hand, this may demonstrate the film's self-reflexive treatment of character, place and genre, given that the typical image of the 'gangster figure', though clearly present in the form of Tae-Sik, remains defamiliarised by a significantly less spectacular, and non-cinematic, landscape. However, one may also argue that Tae-Sik's highly contemporary and hyperbolic appearance is also representative of a specific version or image of Seoul: hyper-modern and, arguably, Westernised. In this particular instance, the film is using Tae-Sik as a vessel to criticise the state of contemporary Seoul, rendering it an impersonal space that is, to a certain extent, divorced from its own rich history and, by extension, its formerly complex identity. In many ways, Tae-Sik and Seoul are synonymous throughout the introductory moments of *The Man from Nowhere*. Both city and city resident, in this instance, are vacuous entities that require transformation.

More importantly, Tae-Sik's technical construction and presentation on screen highlight the occasional isolation of the urban environment. There is an innate spectrality to the character, manifested by various on-screen components. His identity is continuously obscured by either strategically placed mise-en-scene or deliberately evasive cinematography. Often, we must rely on the reactions of other characters to decipher his appearance (Tae-Sik is regularly cut off by the frame, dressed in black and facing away from us). Thus, his phantom-like presence and solitariness within the diegesis are increasingly emphasised. There is a separateness embedded within his being, which effectively compromises both his position within the story-world and the impression he has on the spectator. This is not a character with whom we can immediately sympathise or rely upon and as such, our connection to the narrative remains precarious.

Tae-Sik's own identity (or lack thereof) is further illuminated by the Korean title of the film: *Ahjussi* (which literally translates to 'Mister' or 'Uncle'), and the title with which the film was globally marketed: *The Man from Nowhere*. Both versions demonstrate a sense of anonymity and, more significantly, the absence of place and belonging in relation to one's own surroundings, environment and, in this case, nation state. We know very little of the character's past, only that he may once have had a wife and possibly a child (information that is confirmed in the latter stages of the narrative). The initial lack of any contextual framework here deeply compromises the motives behind Tae-Sik's actions throughout the story. For the majority of the film, he remains an enigma, an outlier and a social anomaly. Regardless of audience expectation, the film refuses to provide any further expositional narration around the character. This means that pivotal pieces of information must be provided to us in an alternative and significantly 'non-Hollywood' manner, namely through Tae-Sik's interactions with other characters and, as previously mentioned, the way in which he influences, and is in turn influenced by, the surrounding cityscape.

He traverses the sub-level plains of Seoul, peripheralising his own existence by refusing to enter into the 'lived' and 'active' spaces of contemporary Korean society—that is until his only acquaintance, a young girl called So-Mi, is kidnapped by drug dealers and, as we later find out, organ harvesters. When the two characters meet, their starkly different realities merge and Tae-Sik must ultimately abandon the self-inflicted peripheral existence that has for so long dictated his social being. It is only from this point of pivotal movement, from one space to another, that the film arguably finds, or inhabits, its true 'genre identity'—in this case, as a gangster text. The entire film is structured into several episodic chase sequences and ultra-violent fights, following Tae-Sik on his relentless journey to find So-Mi. Rarely does the film focus on anything other than this central and highly efficient narrative, which again highlights the industry's ambition to re-establish the fundamentals of the genre and remove any extraneous material or additional story elements. Again, this collectively demonstrates a crucial absence or denial of information—aspects of the narrative that we may expect, but do not necessarily need.

Thus, in its simplest form, *The Man from Nowhere* is a story of 'boy saves girl'. From this summary alone, it is possible to conclude, as Tom Breihan states, that 'none of [the story] is especially original' (Breihan 2017). To a certain extent, this is true and may allude to the Korean film industry's indivisible connections to Hollywood and popular discourse, as well as a growing level of cinematic globalisation. The formulaic trope of the transcendental 'redemption of the anti-hero' (achieved through the character's gradual acceptance of, or affection for, a younger and more fragile being) has been explored many times—recently so in Pierre Morel's *Taken* (2008) and Chad Stahelski's *John Wick* (2014), both of which have enjoyed numerous sequels. Even Luc Besson's *Leon: The Professional* (1994) touches on these themes, though arguably in much more subversive way (which is no doubt a reflection of the French director's unique approach and, more importantly, national cinematic style). However, this text is somewhat of a filmic anomaly (with regard to its French/American hybrid framework and production style) and may not, therefore, prove quite as relevant to this particular observation. When considering films such as *Taken* and *John Wick*, however, one must acknowledge the influence and transnational appeal of Park Chan Wook's *Oldboy* (2003), an earlier text that, through its exploration of a complex father/daughter relationship, subverts both the archetypal gangster figure and the genre in its entirety.

The initial popularity of *Oldboy* and its subsequent status as a 'cult' film significantly shaped the future development of the Korean film industry and its continued engagement with the gangster genre. *The Man from Nowhere* is indicative of this cinematic progression (and is clearly influenced by its cult predecessor in a number of different ways). One might also argue that Hollywood's own response (especially via the release of the *Taken* saga) demonstrates a power shift between the industries. *Oldboy* suggests, in its own inimitable, perverse and idiosyncratic way, that it is possible for the gangster figure to maintain or even desire a familial relationship. This goes against the previous American representations of a typically violent and alienated being, concerned only with maintaining power in a number of homosocial relationships. It is rare for women to sustain any meaningful role in such a male-oriented narrative. Yet, a newly domesticated or family minded portrayal of a classically ungovernable and independent character has recently emerged as a standardised trope in the contemporary Hollywood gangster film, which may be partially due to the pivotal role and cinematic impact of *Oldboy*. However, while a film like *Taken* ultimately solidifies the connection between father and daughter (via a cathartic ending in which Liam Neeson fulfils his role as patriarchal, white saviour), *Oldboy* seeks to destroy this relationship altogether. The eventual revelation of an incestuous encounter (between lead characters Dae-Su and Mi-Do) demonstrates a perversion of, and aversion to, the conventionalised portrait of a heteronormative romance and, more importantly, a rejection of familial ideals.

This demonstrates the layers of self-reflexive subversions that occur and multiply throughout *Oldboy*. By the conclusion of the film, the unfamiliar and the stylistically unconventional aspects of the text become even more extreme. Thus, the film is not only challenging the generic patterns of Hollywood, but it is also questioning its own introductory narrative expectations. By at once championing and ultimately abandoning its own idiosyncratic discourse, *Oldboy* renders the classical gangster story as a filmic tradition prone to boundless stylistic and thematic mutations. This level of reflection, retrospection and self-awareness is integral to the Korean vision of the genre and, indeed, in the way it treats many other modes of popular cinema.

It is also worth noting here that a far less successful American remake of *Oldboy*, directed by Spike Lee, was released in 2013. The domestic and international failure of this text suggests that the two-way relationship between Hollywood and the South Korean film industry, in which narratives and styles are freely exchanged, is only truly beneficial to, and used positively by, the latter party. Korean cinema thrives where Hollywood cannot, mainly through its ability to adopt certain aspects of Western practice and still produce a film that is nationally relevant, socially specific and, above all else, successful. However, when Hollywood attempts to replicate this cinematic manoeuvre with a film such as *Oldboy*, which is intrinsically Korean on every cultural, social and symbolic level, the results are far less satisfactory. Once again, this challenges the previously unparalleled dominance of Hollywood and demonstrates the South Korean film industry's increasing awareness of its globalising competitors, including those in the East, who are more frequently experimenting with American co-productions in the post-millennial era.

When considering the position of *The Man from Nowhere*, one might argue that on the spectrum between East and West, it initially appears to stand closer to the centre. The key differences between *Oldboy* and *The Man from Nowhere*, for instance, are commercialism, coherency and narrative causality. Director Lee Jeong-Beom's text is replete with popular and familiar imagery, recognisable character tropes and an efficient storyline, thus demonstrating an aptitude for Western cinema trends. This does not necessarily mean the film should be aligned alongside, nor considered an extension of, Hollywood. While *The Man from Nowhere* is evidently re-visiting familiar and commercially successful material, it does not completely follow the patterns inaugurated by its recognisable Western counterparts. The formal divergence is maintained not by what we see on screen but in *how* it is presented to us.

As an example, the depiction of the archetypal male gangster inaugurates textual ambiguity. He is a typically generic figure that nevertheless becomes heavily defamiliarised. In *Taken*, *John Wick* and other examples of the Hollywood 'hitman' genre, the overt masculinity of the male protagonist is rarely questioned or scrutinised. His stoic and intensely powerful presentation is immediately established, as is his affinity for violence. As one would perhaps expect, these characteristics only increase with further narrative progress. The distinctive and concrete manifestation of the hyper-masculine figure has become a primary indicative marker of the cinematic 'action' piece—a figure on whom we can rely on to navigate the story-world, re-establish narrative equilibrium and ultimately strengthen patriarchal dominance. From a Western perspective, therefore, the cinematic male 'hero' is unchanging. He is a fixed paradigm and, more importantly, a product of a long-standing patriarchal institution.

It would, of course, be inaccurate to argue that the Korean film industry differs in this regard, as it too has been dominated by male voices and creators from the early Twentieth century through to the new wave period. However, its engagement with, and portrayal of, masculine identity has remained a complex issue, even within the big-budget, mass-consumed and intensely popular films of the post-millennial period (of which *The Man from Nowhere* is a key example). In this particular instance, South Korean cinema challenges the expectations of the 'gangster genre' by directly subverting and questioning that which makes it spectacular and recognisable: the gangster himself. This not only distances the Korean industry from Hollywood, but it also renders any further comparisons with the more generalised 'East Asian' gangster genre redundant. The engagement with, and exploration of, a fragile masculinity is a pivotal marker of differentiation. Neither Hollywood nor the dominant film industries in East Asia have challenged the fundamentals of the cinematic 'anti-hero' in the same way that Korea continuously has (particularly in popular film). The presentation of a deeply fragmented, conflicted and vulnerable masculinity has thus become a major point of polarity between the Korean film industry and its competitors, as well as a tool with which to further contest the representational norms inaugurated by Hollywood.

The Man from Nowhere effectively solidifies these differences via the emphatic and self-reflexive criticism of its leading 'hero'. In comparison to the aforementioned Hollywood protagonists, Tae-Sik is continuously undermined by his own flailing masculinity, vacuous identity and his 'unspecified' position within modern Korean society. He does not immediately align alongside the stoic, powerful and reliable image that one associates with the 'classic gangster'. This further corresponds to Kyung Hyun Kim's argument that in order to instigate the process of 'remasculinization', it is assumed that masculinity has either been lost, severely threatened or was never truly there to begin with—a concept that remains specific to Korean cinematic discourse (Kim 2004). Ultimately, in order for something to be found or 'discovered', it must be assumed, at first, to be missing or lost.

Tae-Sik begins as a lacking or failing character—he embodies a crisis of modern masculinity. As previously discussed, the reason for this is left largely unexplained, which perhaps causes even greater anxiety for both the spectator and the character. It is more concerning because the crisis, the lack and the absence of any discernible origin appear, to some extent, normalised. Unlike *Obaltan*, where problematic masculinity is somewhat justified by the despairing social landscape and contextualised by the postwar experience, Tae-Sik's issues cannot always be rationalised by exterior factors. One can only assume that he represents a culmination of the various impacts of a traumatic, male-oriented history. His position as a symbolic 'masculine enigma' further intensifies both the audience's frustration and, indeed, his own. In retrospect, however, this initial frustration emphasises the character's eventual 'triumph' by the conclusion. A sense of reward is, after all, much greater after a period of failure (and, as previously stated, remasculinisation can only properly and fully occur to the emasculated).

Nevertheless, during the introductory moments of the film, this promise of heroism seems like an impossible outcome, particularly when considering the initial presentation of the character. Tae-Sik is a highly contradictory and inconsistent figure (hence, Confucian masculinity is also immediately undermined). His residence, which is located in a poorer suburb of Seoul, doubles as a pawn shop. However, this business venture is far from successful, as he often exchanges money for items of little value, thus making no profit. Yet, this discreet display of compassion towards his community (and subversive distribution of personal wealth) is, as previously mentioned, juxtaposed with his overall appearance and engagement with the exterior landscape. When Tae-Sik leaves his residence, he is dressed in a sharply tailored, entirely black suit, reminiscent of the modern, business-orientated 'Seoulite' or, indeed, the image of the leading Western action hero.

Ordinarily, such attire would merely satisfy certain expectations of genre. After all, the smartly suited 'Bond-esque' figure is now an instantly identifiable trope. The suit is considered an essential signifier of this specific kind of figure. In this instance, however, it contributes to a troubling impression of the character, especially when it is revealed that he is dressed in such a way because of a recent visit to his wife's memorial. Therefore, the suit functions in a number of different ways. On the one hand, it is used to signify respect, tradition and sentimentality (which subverts the ubiquitous, hyper-masculinised image associated with the gangster archetype). On the other hand, and perhaps more significantly, the suit acts as a marker of the character's desire to integrate himself into what is now a quasi-capitalist nation. Collectively, these narrative intricacies may also allude to the state of Korean society itself, in which the 'economic system is capitalist ... the social structure socialist and mindsets are communist' (Kim 2014). Evidently, Tae-Sik is as contradictory as the place in which he exists. He has manifested a façade to conceal his true identity or, indeed, his Korean identity—that is his personal connection to a national past. In this respect, his image aligns with the dominant view of the urban space in which he belongs—Seoul. Often, from a global, exterior perspective, the city is simultaneously presented to us and perceived as an increasingly modern, transnational landscape (and thus focuses on concerns of cultural diminishment). While this presentation is certainly valid, it is a distanced and objective impression of Seoul and therefore does not take into account the deeper national connections that remain embedded within the city and amongst its residents.

Tae-Sik's presentation functions in a similar way. Outwardly or superficially, he satisfies a certain kind of image, one that is linked to affluence, capitalism or, from a purely filmic perspective, the generic action hero. His actual state of living, however, which includes a fairly menial job, creates an altogether different narrative, one that juxtaposes his physical presentation on screen. Inevitably, one must doubt to what extent Tae-Sik remains authentically Korean—the same question that a globalising Seoul continuously faces. Fundamentally, the character's appearance, disposition and very existence are shaped by the cityscape and the views of a metropolitan society. However, this also may be a postmodern and self-conscious technique employed by the film to criticise the aforementioned, standardised approaches to the genre (and, perhaps, further emphasise Tae-Sik's transformation by the conclusion of the film). In these introductory moments, *The Man from Nowhere* is clearly declaring both its affinity to and frustration with the Westernised interpretations of the gangster character and the clinical world he often represents. In some ways, Tae-Sik is a simulation or a reproduction of a popular filmic motif as he fulfils the stereotypical and superficial role of the gangster. As the narrative unfolds, however, it becomes clear that his simulative presentation is designed to contradict and temporarily disguise that which is far from conventional—namely his conflicted masculine identity.

As the character moves through the city, his initial image slowly starts to unravel, illuminating both the psychological, 'Koreanised' complexities of Tae-Sik and the solitary uniqueness of Seoul. The ordinariness and familiarity that is established in the beginning function as a means of exaggerating the film's gradual subversion of plot, character and space. Collectively, however, this makes Tae-Sik and the film itself highly unreliable and unpredictable, as there is no clear point at which this deconstructive, 'Korean' discourse emerges. Thus, the spectator's ability to 'read' Tae-Sik's identity (and subsequent masculinity) is dependent on a number of 'diegetic variables'—namely his relationship with the city, with other characters and the way in which they influence his own transcendental journey. Initially, it appears that this concern is remedied in yet another ostensibly generic way: through the introduction of So-Mi, the young girl who lives nearby. However, it quickly becomes apparent that she too serves a greater and intrinsic narrative function.

During the first quarter of the film, the story establishes a pivotal connection between these two main characters. They remain inextricably linked via their similar placement within both the urban and domestic spaces of the film. They live in close proximity to each other, in the same building: Tae-Sik on the central floor and So-Mi on the base level, with her negligent and drug-addicted Mother. The former's residence is particularly symbolic as it positions Tae-Sik in a purgatorial zone. He literally exists halfway between the presumably more expensive and 'open' floors above, and the dark, claustrophobic confinements below. The allusions to a contemporary, urbanised heaven and hell are used in this instance to further highlight the duality of the character and his fragmented masculinity. While the use of the term 'purgatory' may seem ill-fitting in this scenario, given that it is a predominantly Christian concept (and ideas of Korean Confucianism contribute substantially to this chapter), it aptly describes Tae-Sik's social and psychological position—trapped between worlds, in a state of limbo. Purgatory in this instance is not used in the religious sense. Instead, it symbolically highlights the dichotomy between Tae-Sik's past and present self, and his inability to find an equilibrium. The building in which he lives further emphasises this interior conflict.

So-Mi, meanwhile, remains confined to the floors below and, more importantly, is conditioned by the sub-levels of the cityscape—the transgressive, sinister and 'hidden' spaces that are intentionally peripheralised by the vibrant and touristic gaze on the contemporary metropolis. There is a sense that this is the 'Seoul' we are not supposed to see, but it is still entirely relevant because of So-Mi. For a cinema that has so often been characterised by its historic marginalisation of the female voice and feminine identity (particularly within popular film, both on and off the cinema screen), *The Man from Nowhere* places a surprising level of symbolic meaning on So-Mi, however fleeting her physical presence is within the storyworld (Paquet 2017). There is a certain amount of power entrenched within the character—she exists as the primary emotive catalyst of the film. Even though it is possible to argue that So-Mi functions merely as a 'vehicle' for transition and change to occur within Tae-Sik, his dependence on her is instrumental in the formation of his own masculine and, more importantly, *Korean* identity. This inaugurates a complex and, perhaps, unexpected discourse of gender relations in Korean cinema, which becomes especially significant when considering the typically male-driven models of the gangster narrative (at least for those associated with Hollywood).

So-Mi's influence on the development of Tae-Sik's masculinity (and patriarchal responsibility) challenges the previous representations of female place, space and voice in the genre. His identity is not merely an autonomous, self-cultivated extension of an independent psyche. It is instead portrayed as a by-product of his relationship with another, significantly more self-assured, female figure. So-Mi is also a very young character, which suggests that Tae-Sik's issues are generational—they infer a broader crisis of adulthood. Despite her impoverished living conditions, lack of education and temperamental relationship with her Mother, So-Mi displays a worldliness, self-awareness and heightened 'sense of self' that far eclipse Tae-Sik's narrow views and solitary outlook. While it is possible to argue that this construction of the female character is merely used to counteract the heavy drama and complexity of her male counterpart, it may also symbolise or allude to the younger generations as a force for seismic change (and as such renders the stasis/crisis of masculinity as a generational matter). Ultimately, So-Mi dictates the movement and progress of the diegetic world, as well as the movement of Tae-Sik as a developing figure. Without her, the world of the film, and everything contained within it, cannot sustain meaning.

In relation to Tae-Sik and his floundering masculinity, So-Mi is as threatening as she is nurturing. From her presence alone, she is able to disturb the patriarchal order—a significant feat when considering the largely male-dominated landscape in which the film takes place. Even when she is not physically present on screen, her 'aura' haunts the diegetic world, stylistically and symbolically. Her story is told vicariously through Tae-Sik, whose actions, which become increasingly volatile, often parallel the danger she faces. Though we may not regularly see So-Mi, our desperation to find/locate her mirrors the urgency of both the narrative and Tae-Sik's development. She remains visible not in the literal sense but in the emotional sense, conditioning every formal and thematic turn of the story and, ultimately, our response to it.

More importantly, So-Mi is also utilised as a tool with which to criticise the aforementioned 'hyper-masculinity' of a crime-riddled Seoul and its increasingly apathetic residents, including Tae-Sik. This is evidenced during the scene in which an affluent Mother and her son accuse So-Mi of stealing. When the police eventually become involved in the dispute, they ask her if she is with a parent. So-Mi points hopefully to Tae Sik, who has been silently observing from a distance. As the police approach, he walks away, rejecting both So-Mi and his ostensible role as the 'Father figure'. More than just a criticism of class polarity in South Korea, this crucial scene also presents the seismic flaws and narrowed vision of a social system predominantly created and sustained by men. There is no semblance of duty, honour or redemption here, only a profound sense of failure: the failure of fathers, brothers and sons, failure of the patriarchal system and the failure of men.

This criticism ultimately compromises both the 'likeability' of the character and his potential for emotional growth. To establish a figure on whom the spectator cannot bestow any immediate empathy or affection defies popular discourse, particularly for a genre that so heavily relies on a charismatic leading protagonist. More importantly, Tae-Sik's unwillingness or, indeed, incapability of being a 'Father', 'protector' and 'provider' (to So-Mi) once again calls into question the legitimacy of the neo-Confucian expectations to which he, whether knowingly or otherwise, remains inextricably bound. While he is clearly an intensely modern character, Tae-Sik still remains burdened by tradition and the threat of a dominant masculinity left unfulfilled. Yet, the film refuses to completely eschew the continued importance of these expectations and concepts. Even though *The Man from Nowhere* is a highly contemporary text, it still engages with key historical ideologies and thought processes when regarding the purpose and narrative function of its two main protagonists. This demonstrates, as Richard Howson and Brian Yecies observe, a prevailing comprehension of modern Korea as a 'neo-Confucian culture' in which it is 'impossible to understand gender relations and their hegemonic operation [as] disconnected from tradition' (Howson and Yecies 2015, p. 14). Both masculinity and femininity appear deeply intertwined with certain cultural philosophies and an enduring patriarchal discourse, to such an extent that, even now, it is difficult to consider one concept in complete isolation from the other.

This presents, rather controversially, a return to a specific set of social expectations within *The Man from Nowhere*. Unlike *Obaltan*, which sees the main protagonist Cheolho despair at, hold contempt for and ultimately abandon his 'Confucian role', Tae-Sik's journey is designed to achieve the exact opposite. In rescuing So-Mi, the character is able to re-establish his own Confucian identity and hierarchical position, albeit in a subversive and highly idiosyncratic way. By the conclusion, he fully occupies the aforementioned role of 'Father' and 'protector'. Yet, the ideas addressed here do not possess the same gravity or cultural and historical significance (when compared to a text like *Obaltan*). They are not designed to be read or interpreted in the same way, mainly because masculine identity is not something to be feared or a concept that induces anxiety. It is instead a flawed system that is capable of growth and repair—it cultivates a realm of progress. In *The Man from Nowhere*, the acknowledgement of Confucian ideals, whether problematic or otherwise, is merely used to emphasise the development of the character and, ultimately, provide a coherent narrative resolution.

Violent Spaces: Re-examining the 'Fight Scene'

When considering the aforementioned focus on the 'male body' in the Korean gangster film, *The Man from Nowhere* takes the exploration of male physicality further by drawing attention to the relationship between Tae-Sik's changing appearance and his evolving emotional state. The narrative revolves around certain stages of his physical development. Essentially, there is an episodic function to the presentation of his body and his interaction with it. Indeed, the film maintains a unique focus on the body and what it represents—pain, punishment, longing and, finally, redemption. This is evidenced from the beginning of the film, when So-Mi paints a face on Tae-Sik's fingernail. Though clearly a less extreme example, the imprint affects Tae-Sik in the same way that Cheolho's toothache does in *Obaltan*—it is a constant reminder of the pain he must endure and, ultimately, accept as part of his own identity. In this instance, the body may also be considered as a site of anxiety or as a canvas upon which the memories of historical trauma can unfold. So-Mi's imprint on Tae-Sik not only acts as a reminder of the connection they share, but it also acts as a broader symbol of the character's guilt and the inherent torment that is embedded within his personal memories (which is, in retrospect, intensified upon the discovery of the death of his child).

The bodily themes continue throughout the film, when in one scene Tae-Sik decides to cut his own hair (and his painted fingernail is notably visible as he holds the scissors). The scene marks an integral point of transition for the character, physically, symbolically and psychologically. By cutting his hair, he is ridding himself of his immediate former life and identity. More importantly, he is stepping away from the solitary spaces within the diegesis that, up until this point, have conditioned his existence. The haircut is short, revealing and simple (close to what is expected of Korean men when they enter the army), and signifies a level of self-acceptance. The image of Tae-Sik in this moment may well be a reflection of his younger, past self and additionally act as reminder, albeit superficially, of his return to a predominantly Confucian identity, re-assuming his role as patriarchal saviour and, on some level, military hero.

Shortly after, the camera stays focused on Tae-Sik as he stares at his reflection in the mirror. The duality of his character is made evident in this prolonged and contemplative moment. By this point, he has essentially solidified his commitment to So-Mi. There is a conflation of two different realities here, two different beings and two opposing histories. Each fragment or 'version' is needed to re-establish or rediscover Tae-Sik's masculinity. The emphasis on the body and the concept of pain are also apparent, as the injuries that the character has sustained up until this point are highlighted on his torso (via backlighting that casts an ethereal glow around him). This creates an otherworldly, angelic impression of the body, effectively ridding Tae-Sik of his previous sins, which have largely been manifested through his neglect of So-Mi. The connection between religion and the body is not especially unique here (in the sense that gangsters are often rendered as 'god-like' on screen), but it does allude to a heightened sense of transformation, transcendence and redemption taking place within the character. The acute focus on Tae-Sik's body persists throughout the entirety of the film, particularly during the fight sequences, which both form and preserve the narrative integrity and structure of the text.

Whether in the traditional, less affluent outskirts of Seoul, or the inner city, frenetic club scene, many of the urban spaces interrogated within *The Man from Nowhere* feel and appear distinctly Korean. That is, however, until the major fight sequences. These violent events occur within spaces that do not appear culturally, nationally or historically specific. They are vacant, purgatorial and unassuming stages, designed to foreground the ensuing conflict between Tae-Sik and his enemies. Furthermore, by purposefully highlighting the unspecified and vacuous nature of these spaces (i.e. a public bathroom), the narrative is instead focusing on Tae-Sik and his ability to take control of his own identity and journey. After each fight, the character is, to some extent, 'reborn' (and closer to a reunion with So-Mi); thus, he can then re-enter the lived spaces of Korean society. Essentially, every violent encounter functions as a subversive rite of passage.

The final fight sequence in particular is a crucial moment in the story, mostly because it functions as a cathartic reminder of Tae-Sik's conclusive transformation. Setting, again, is key, as unlike the other spaces explored throughout the film, the room in which Tae-Sik must face his determinate enemies is decidedly non-Korean. The space is palatial, with stone pillars, marble floors and statues of Ancient Greek persuasion, and bears no resemblance to the hyper-urbanised settings explored previously in the text. It appears completely out of time and place, a spatial anomaly that clearly juxtaposes with its inhabitants and their current situation. Both Tae-Sik and his many opponents are all dressed either in black or white—a starkly modern contrast to the gold opulence and aura of myth that pervades the room. This is clearly a space of finality and decision, as is evidenced within the shot below.

While the altercation initially starts with heavy gunfire, the means of attack is soon reduced to hand-to-hand combat and intensely vicious knife play. Once again, this not only results in several close-up shots of the 'male body' (which instigates a level of gender subversive objectification), but it also emphasises the extent to which said body can endure immediate physical and emotional pain. The notion of 'body horror' is a concept that Korean cinema regularly explores, and often very successfully, particularly within films that invite religious/existential readings, that is Park Chan Wook's *Thirst* (2009) and Na Hong Jin's *The Wailing* (2016). While this may be designed to acknowledge broader Asian cinematic trends and 'complement the concreteness of local sensibilities with the ambiguity of global tastes', as Laikwan Pang observes, in the case of *The Man from Nowhere*, it still feels like a naturally integrated step in the narrative (Pang 2011, p. 160). 'Extreme' cinema, in this instance, is not a result of stereotyping or 'othering' (by the West). Rather, it is a fully functional component within the story. In this final fight, the figures become visually monstrous, bloody and, with the exception of Tae-Sik, come to resemble something far from human. In addition to being a highly stylised and seamlessly edited sequence, this particular fight adopts a sinister and graphic edge, especially when it is assumed by Tae-Sik (and, by extension, the audience) that So-Mi has been killed. Memory, trauma and guilt once again occupy a clear position throughout the fight, and the potential loss of So-Mi is the rationale needed to ultimately justify the hyper-violent nature of the scene.

Collectively, the quick succession of shots is paralleled with the construction and development of the scene itself. As Tae-Sik sustains more injuries, the speed of editing increases, creating a flurry of obstructive cuts that gradually immerse the spectator within the action. On several occasions, the camera inhabits Tae-Sik's perspective so that his position is synonymous with our own. This is in direct contrast to the beginning of the film, in which we are immediately distanced from the character, guided through the diegetic world from an objective stance. Evidently, the film has gradually manipulated the space between spectator and screen here, so that, ultimately, Tae-Sik's gaze mirrors our own.

More importantly, the use of knives and bodily contact in this scene act as a direct rejection of the stylistic paradigms of the genre. Ordinarily and, perhaps, historically, the action sequence has often been characterised by its sensationalised usage of guns, especially within the Western and gangster genres. In Hollywood, this is to be expected, as it clearly acknowledges America's long-standing and controversial relationship with gun violence. In *The Man from Nowhere*, however, the formerly ubiquitous nature of guns is replaced by the desire to establish close proximity between cinematic enemies. Not only does this break down stylistic and aesthetic norms, but it also illuminates the way in which the film augments a present, aggressive and confrontational masculinity. In this instance, physical contact and violent homosocial encounters equate to some form of self-validation. Guns are rendered useless because they create distance and separation between each participant, making it more difficult to capture the sacrificial nature of a fight. After all, knives typically lead to a higher level of graphic bloodshed and bodily contact.

One must also acknowledge the *type* of knife that is used by each character throughout the sequence. Tae-Sik's final opponent, a highly skilled, non-Korean assassin, notably uses a weapon with a curved blade—a 'Karambit' knife of Indonesian design. Ordinarily, such a minute detail would seem inconsequential. Here, however, in a fight scene which foregrounds the specific, cinematic and even artistic use of knives, and renders such objects as integral to the formal and thematic structure of the entire sequence, one cannot overlook the relevance of the assassin's weapon of choice. By contrast, this is especially important when considering the knife that Tae-Sik uses: a straight, plain, narrow blade that has no clear national or cultural connections. Even during the latter stages of the film, the character is still denied a complete and coherent identity. Similar to the weapon he relies upon to navigate and overcome the violent diegetic world, Tae-Sik is also bereft of any concrete origins (and hence remains, up until this point, the 'man from nowhere'). Evidently, the mise-en-scene within this scene functions to position the cultural parameters and background of each character and, as a result, further isolate Tae-Sik.

By this stage, however, the character's alienation may not be perceived as a negative outcome. Ultimately, his absence of identity not only manifests a sense of freedom in this scene, but it also distances him from his on-screen counterparts—versions of the hyper-masculine figure that are arguably much more generic, one-dimensional and, by extension, problematic. There are several instances, for example, wherein the action is temporarily halted in order for Tae-Sik to establish eye-contact with his enemy. A perverse kind of mirroring takes place here, as the character must face a potential version of himself—an identity that he may well have succumbed to had he not found purpose or, in this particular instance, the self-affirming character of So-Mi (who acts as the all-important 'daughter' figure). Therefore, *The Man from Nowhere* is not necessarily about finding one's physical place and space, or even locating masculine identity in relation to the cultural and national landscape. Even though these concepts occupy a substantial part of Tae-Sik's personal narrative, they do not condition his journey in its entirety. Instead, the text questions the malleability or, indeed, adaptability of structures, ideologies and thought processes that already exist, both textually (in terms of genre identity) and symbolically/socially (in terms of Confucian beliefs and familial relationships).

Conclusion: A Return to Confucian Sensibility?

While *Obaltan* and *The Man from Nowhere* are texts that both address Korean masculinity in equal measure, they have drastically different conclusions. Where the former emphasises national/masculine hopelessness and the futile nature of preserving certain Korean systems, the latter attempts to redefine what these systems are and ultimately restore their relevance in a contemporary setting. This is made plain within the narrative arc of the film and, in particular, the concluding scene. After Tae-Sik has rescued So-Mi, we return to the neighbourhood in which both characters were originally introduced, which essentially provides a cyclical moment of revelation and exposition. Re-visiting this familiar space is a crucial moment within the narrative and is a cathartic step for the now bruised, but enlightened, Tae-Sik. He is not a different man by this point, only improved, and this aura of transformation is simultaneously projected onto the landscape that surrounds his former home. The area no longer resembles the dark, impoverished and claustrophobic space established at the beginning of the film, despite the disturbance of several police cars and many curious onlookers. The two characters are captured in mid-wide shot, holding hands under the sunlight, standing in front of the familiar convenience store (now a subversive sanctuary for So-Mi) and its bemused owner.

Every area of the diegesis has been replenished and every corner of the neighbourhood restored, in both the cinematic and symbolic sense, which coincides with Graham Gillespie's reading of 'the representation of urban space' in the Korean gangster text, which often functions as 'the physical horizon of [the protagonist's] lived experience' (Gillespie 2016, p. 64). Essentially, the landscape runs parallel to the personal journey of the gangster figure. During the final moments in *The Man from Nowhere*, there are no more oblique camera angles, obscured faces or imposing urban facades. To a certain extent, the street is *normalised*, so that a different kind of reality has been introduced to us. Perhaps this suggests that, in the end, the city is portrayed as a space designed to 'reverse-liberate', which, in this instance, means restoring the 'status quo' and returning to the stability of the past. The characters are, after all, back in the place in which they started—an area of the city that remains untouched by modernisation and globalisation. Furthermore, both Tae-Sik and So-Mi have, in this final stage, reacquired their Confucian roles as 'father' and 'daughter', but this is not depicted as a negative resolution. On the contrary, the return to traditional relationships and familial duties here equates to a sense of deliverance (hence the aforementioned 'reverse-liberation').

When considering Tae-Sik's appearance in these concluding moments, one can clearly identify the transformative process that has occurred. This is to be expected, given the continued focus on his body throughout the film. As previously mentioned, his shorter hair allows his facial expressions to be easily read and suggests personal acceptance of his own identity. The scars and bruises on his body act as reminders of his redemptive journey, and the pain they inflict, like Cheolho in *Obaltan*, reaffirms the character's existence. The suit, a former motif of quasi-capitalism and Western dominance, is now worn and dirtied with dried blood. Similar to other subversions of generic mise-en-scene, this also demonstrates a breakdown of representational norms. In this instance, the suit, once a primary trope of the genre and the gangster archetype (as previously established), is essentially rendered useless because it no longer satisfies Tae-Sik's 'remasculinized' image. It no longer contributes to Tae-Sik's identity or, more importantly, conditions the spectator's impression of him. Instead, the primary focus remains on Tae-Sik's body—specifically, his hands. Even after the turbulent events of the protagonist's journey, So-Mi's nail art remains as a vivid shot of bright yellow. This is, after all, the only constant that truly matters.

When Tae Sik and So-Mi say their final goodbye, it appears that positive equilibrium has been established. More importantly, there is the continued sense of hope—hope for the future, for the next generation and for the aforementioned 'national male subject'. The last shot is, inevitably, of Tae-Sik: an extreme close-up of his face as he hugs So-Mi. The manner in which he is captured in these concluding moments is significantly different to his introduction. When we first see Tae-Sik, he is an intensely elusive figure, not only to us but also to the diegetic world from which he is emotionally disconnected. He is shot from a distance, off-centre, almost out of frame entirely—a marked contrast to the intimate final image, in which his face occupies the majority of the screen. Indeed, these final few moments radically change our impression of not only the character but also the film itself. The increasing presence of sentimentality, of reflection and remorse, is reminiscent of a melodrama. No longer does the film adhere to the limitations and expectations of the gangster or action text. Graham Gillespie observes how the continued application of genre hybridity in the Korean gangster text, in which there is a desire to 'diversify or variate from standard genre fare', offers 'opportunities for gangster heroes to be represented as unscrupulous winners rather than tragic losers', which, again, highlights the restorative nature of contemporary masculine identity in such narratives (Gillespie 2016, p. 63).

The Man from Nowhere is no exception to this rule. Ultimately, Tae-Sik 'wins' when he accepts his bittersweet position as father figure and thus acknowledges his Confucian responsibilities. While he may have started as an 'unscrupulous' figure (so as to initially satisfy the generic boundaries of the genre), as the narrative progresses, his purpose and function within the story-world move far beyond the paradigmatic boundaries linked to the typical 'gangster text'. By the conclusion, his character, and the film itself, provides a crucial viewpoint on the state of contemporary Korean masculinity and the systems that continue to condition it. Even with this newly acquired knowledge, however, one must acknowledge the film's overt idealism in these final moments. Ultimately, Tae-Sik's character satisfies a noble and romantic vision of Korean male identity (and thus reveals the collective desires of a patriarchal society in an age of post-trauma). Regardless of how persuasive this image is, however, it is still indicative of Korean cinema's 'hope of recovering a wholesome maleness and purity from a fantasy, as if it can be transposed to be absolutely real' (Kim 2004, p. 26). Of course, whether this act of transposition is at all possible is a dilemma that remains largely unsolved.

REFERENCES

Breihan, T. 2017. In South Korea, A Horrifically Extreme Thriller can be the Box Office Champion of the Year. *AV Club*. Accessed 15 April 2019. https://www.avclub.com/in-south-korea-a-horrifically-extreme-thriller-can-be-1805660477.

Chung, S. 2016. To Have or To be? Narrating Confucian Value in Contemporary Korea. *International Communication of Chinese Culture* 3 (4): 631–643. https://doi.org/10.1007/s40636-016-0068-8.

Gillespie, G.N. 2016. Reading the 'New World': Neoliberalism in the South Korean Gangster Film. *Journal of Japanese and Korean Cinema: Korean Screen Culture* 8 (1): 59–72. https://doi.org/10.1080/17564905.2016.1171567.

Howson, R., and B. Yecies. 2015. Korean Cinema's Female Writers-Directors and the Hegemony of Men. *Gender a Výzkum* 16 (1): 14–22. https://doi.org/10.13060/12130028.2015.16.1.167.

Jeong, K. 2006. Nation Rebuilding and Postwar South Korean Cinema: *The Coachman* and *The Stray Bullet*. *Journal of Korean Studies* 11 (1): 129–162. https://doi.org/10.1353/jks.2006.0007.

Jin, Y. 2016. The Issue of Gender Equality in Confucian Culture. *The London School of Economics and Political Science*. Accessed 27 August 2020. https://blogs.lse.ac.uk/gender/2016/01/18/the-issue-of-gender-equality-in-confucian-culture.

Kim, K. 2004. *The Remasculinization of Korean Cinema*. Durham: Duke University Press.

Kim, S. 2014. Is Korea a Capitalist Country? *The Korea Herald*. Accessed 26 September 2019. http://www.koreaherald.com/view.php?ud=20141118001115.

Kim, S. 2018. Jung Doo-Hong and the Gangster Body: Kkangpae in Contemporary South Korean Cinema. In *A Companion to the Gangster Film*, ed. George S. Larke-Walsh, 510–512. Oxford: Wiley-Blackwell.

Leong, A. 2004. Injadong Sajong Bolgeot Eobda/Nowhere to Hide. In *The Cinema of Japan and Korea*, ed. Justin Bower, 181–187. London: Wallflower.

Myonggu, Y., and W.A. Douglas. 1967. Korean Confucianism Today. *Pacific Affairs* 40 (1): 43–59. https://doi.org/10.2307/2754621.

Pang, L. 2011. New Asian Cinema and its Circulation of Violence. *Modern Chinese Literature and Culture* 17 (1): 159–187.

Paquet, D. 2017. The (Few) Women Breaking through in Korean Cinema. *BFI*. Accessed 3 October 2019. https://www.bfi.org.uk/news-opinion/sight-sound-magazine/features/women-korean-cinema.

Park, A.H., and M. Joon. 2017. Daehan Neo-Realism and the Conundrum of Aimless Confucianism in Yu Hyun Mok's *Obaltan* (1961). *Journal of Japanese and Korean Cinema* 9 (2): 90–106. https://doi.org/10.1080/17564905.2017.1368138.

Tikhonov, V. 2007. Masculinizing the Nation: Gender Ideologies in Traditional Korea and in the 1890s–1900s Korean Enlightenment Discourse. *The Journal of Asian Studies* 66 (4): 1029–1065. https://doi.org/10.1017/S0021911807001283.

Walsh, G. 2018. *A Companion to the Gangster Film*. Oxford: Wiley-Blackwell.

CHAPTER 5

The Suppressive City

Narratives of masculinity and the male experience have, historically, prevailed in South Korean film, both in front of and behind the camera. As Richard Howard and Brian Yecies argue, 'it is no exaggeration to say that in Korea, masculinity and men are privileged', and this has resulted in the implementation of a 'gender bias' throughout many forms of popular media and culture (Howard and Yecies 2015, p. 17). Thus far within this book, and particularly within the preceding chapter, it has been established that the portrayal of Korean national identity (alongside its expansive narratives of memory and trauma) remains deeply connected and, in some cases, inextricably bound to the psychology of the male subject. This discourse has been further sustained by a Korean media landscape dominated by men (particularly since the economic boom of the 1990s). Darcy Paquet observes how, 'within a highly competitive and cutthroat [film] industry', the presence of female directors, whilst certainly apparent, remains a peripheral issue and is repeatedly overshadowed by the varied successes of six male auteurs: Park Chan-Wook, Hong Sangsoo, Bong Joon-ho, Lee Chang-dong, Kim Ki-Duk and Kim Jee-Woon (Paquet 2017). As a result, it is commonly understood that since the new wave period, 'producers and investors are uncomfortable entrusting large budgets to women directors', especially when there are already established (male) filmmakers who are likely to deliver film texts that are commercially and critically successful, on both a domestic and international level (Paquet 2017). The very recent success of Bong Joon Ho's *Parasite* supports this hypothesis (given the gradual yet assured trajectory of the director's profile) and stands as a significant addition to a string of successful post-millennial Korean texts that are created by men and largely feature male-oriented narratives.

This is not to say that we should discredit or question the accomplishments of these male auteurs. Nor does it necessarily imply that they, or their work, should be viewed as redundant or as part of a conservative, static or, indeed, problematic film culture. On the contrary, each filmmaker has been an invaluable asset to the overall development of the South Korean film industry, particularly within the periods immediately preceding and following the millennium. We must also acknowledge the extent to which the industry, as a broad, cultural institution, has acted as an extension of Korean society and, more importantly, has reflected certain national ideologies. Rather than criticise the individuals that collectively, yet perhaps unknowingly or unintentionally, perpetuate the gender divide in the Korean film workspace, one must instead analyse the wider systems, structures and historical narratives that have led to this divide (within both standard industry practices and within the Korean film texts these practices produce or manifest). It is also worth noting that, in some cases, and particularly within the work of Lee Chang Dong, the representation of Korean women covers a substantial narrative space, especially in films such as *Oasis* (2002), *Poetry* (2010) and *Secret Sunshine* (2007). Therefore, to completely dismiss this catalogue of work would prove to be an entirely reductive exercise. Together, these directors have made a significant contribution to the Korean cinematic landscape *and* to the overarching reputation of South Korean film as a site of textual subversion, experimentation and, most significantly, national and/or cultural relevance.

However, it cannot be doubted that these achievements have, to a large extent, been abetted by gendered occupations and attitudes. This goes far beyond the film texts themselves, and in light of the movements taking place across global film industries, namely towards gender equality, one cannot ignore the striking and questionable absence of women in this Korean filmmaking canon. The narratives of success embedded within the new wave period remain heavily masculinised. While there are women working actively within the industry, mainly as producers and script writers, there remains a prominent imbalance with regard to the attention they receive, the acknowledgement they are given and the spaces they occupy.

If the commercial aesthetic of post-millennial South Korean cinema was, and continues to be, a product or extension of the nation's ruling patriarchy, the only means of entry into the film market for female creatives, as previously noted by Paquet, is often through independent, smaller-scale projects.

This is the case for Jeong Jae-Eun's *Take Care of My Cat*, released in 2001. While the film was not initially successful, it attracted a larger audience (and subsequently gained more attention worldwide) in the years that followed. At present, the film is recognised as an important text in the industry's small, but growing, anthology of films that are directed by women and feature female-oriented narratives. Progress remains steady but sure, which suggests that there is an increasing appetite, from domestic audiences, to see stronger, more complex, more frequent and, frankly, *better* representations of Korean women not only in film but also within other forms of popular, contemporary entertainment. Ultimately, this is a national issue, especially given the country's developing reputation as a cultural powerhouse.

This advancing status has, of course, been greatly motivated, altered and informed by the modern Korean consumer. Fan culture occupies a significant space in the realm of entertainment in South Korea and can often prove to be a source of controversy (especially when considered alongside the music industry and the world of celebrity). In his discussion of the Korean pop industry and the new wave cultural movement, or 'Hallyu' as it is alternatively known, Timothy Gitzen notes how 'consumers, or fans, have a certain degree of power that they can actively wield', and this has created an interdependent dialogue between industry and audience within the entertainment sector (Gitzen 2013, p. 7). Due to various technological advances, increased usage of social media and the rise of 'fan service' (where Korean celebrities take extra steps to connect with their admirers), the pop-culture consumer continues to have a pronounced impact on both the movement and progress of the entertainment landscape as a whole and the individuals who rely on it and/or work within it.

At present, it is very easy for fans to have their voices heard and directly engage with certain companies—particularly in an era of social media dominance. The intense and, at times, obsessive fan culture in South Korea can be highly problematic, as those working within the industry are heavily scrutinised on a regular basis (and again, this remains quite specific to pop-music performers). However, in the instance of South Korean cinema, the criticism is not quite as ubiquitous or, indeed, aggressive. Audience response is often used constructively, as is evidenced when analysing the reaction to *Take Care of My Cat*, whereby a number of avid admirers of the film worked together, collectively campaigned and gave it a second life—one that extended far beyond the cinema screen (Seong 2003). Ultimately, the voices of the 'fandom', many of whom were notably from Incheon (a city in which the text is partially set), allowed the film to have an extended theatrical release and, more importantly, propelled it into the wider and more globalised circle of Korean popular culture. Latterly, *Take Care of My Cat* was also a featured film at the 2016 London Korean Film Festival (LKFF), in a special event entitled 'The Lives of Korean Women Through the Eyes of Women Directors'.[1] This suggests that the interest in Korean female narratives is not limited to the domestic realm but part of a universal enquiry. There is now a collective, pan-national desire to investigate the role of women in Korean popular culture and understand why representations of female identity have remained marginalised for so long and/or historically conceptualised by male directors alone.

Naturally, as the popularity of South Korean cinema grows, especially within the post-*Parasite* era, so too does the scrutiny of its key industry practices. *Take Care of my Cat* was arguably one of the first female-centric texts, in the new wave period, that initiated this global acknowledgement of the importance of portraying and, indeed, celebrating Korean women on screen. This gradual shifting of attitudes and exposure is significant, particularly if we are to consider the previous iterations of Korean women in cinema throughout the mid- to late Twentieth century (which were created by men and thus act as a reflection of a dominant patriarchy). Now, alongside Jeong Jae-Eun, there are number of female directors that have achieved notable success on the film festival circuit, namely Yim Soon-Rye (*Forever the Moment*, 2008), Park Chan-Ok (*Paju*, 2009) and Lee Kyoung-Mi (*Crush and Blush*, 2008). Together, their films have privileged the female experience and, more importantly, presented female identity as something inherently complex, multi-layered and, above all else, deeply national.

---

[1] Information provided by http://koreanfilm.co.uk/site/discover-more/festival-archive/the-2016-festival/the-2016-programme/special-focus-the-lives-of-korean-women-through-the-eyes-of-women-directors. Accessed 26th March 2020.

Transgression and a Threat to the Confucian Order: Representations of the Korean Woman in the Mid- to Late Twentieth Century

As in the previous chapter of this book (which largely focused on narratives of masculinity and nationhood), one must inevitably reflect on and analyse the historical timeline of Korean cinema to further understand how and why these distinctive representations of gender identity have emerged in the post-millennial age. It appears that the current trend (inaugurated by female directors) of narratives revolving around contemporary girlhood is not simply a response to the long-standing marginalisation of Korean women in cinema but also an emphatic critique of existing representations, rare as they are (and this further highlights the need to understand contemporary Korean cinema as a *reactionary* body of work). One of the most famous or, indeed, notorious, cinematic portrayals of Korean womanhood is in Kim Ki Young's *The Housemaid* (1960), a landmark text released in the 'Golden Age' of South Korean filmmaking. The film, which follows the gradual ruination of a nuclear family when a transgressive femme fatale is introduced into the domestic space, is continually cited as a strong influence not only for current Korean directors but also for a number of American filmmakers.

There is no denying that *The Housemaid* is an important film. Its radical approach to style, tone and technical execution subverts the paradigms of the hybrid genre with which it is ostensibly associated: the melodramatic thriller. It was unlike anything else released at the time and for this fact alone, it will always remain a pivotal contribution to South Korea's broader cultural timeline. However, while the film is rightly regarded as a noteworthy, meaningful and highly influential text (in terms of its form, its appearance and its rejection of classical narrative), in retrospect, it still validates certain hegemonic approaches to gender. As Kyung Hyun Kim notes, 'despite the casting of the maid as the central character whose psychological complications add depth to the story, *The Housemaid* is undoubtedly a masculine drama', mainly because it upholds the dominant cinematic and ideological narratives of the period (Kim 2004, p. 241).

Ultimately, the male protagonist of the film and head of the family, Dong-Sik, is the centrifugal figure around which all narrative elements revolve; thus, his experience within the diegetic landscape is privileged and significantly focalised. He is the figure with whom the audience is supposed to sympathise and ideologically align. Therefore, *The Housemaid* remains a male-centric text, designed to satiate the expectations of an equally male-centric society. The story-world of the film is highly insular, in both a pragmatic and symbolic sense. Not only does it take place, almost entirely, within the confines of a single, two-storey household (a visual nod to the encroachment of Western modernisation), but there is also the sense that the wider properties of Dong-Sik's body, mind and spirit are embedded within the space, in the very infrastructure of the building in which he resides. Therefore, any exterior threat to this space acts, by extension, as a threat to him (and, perhaps, to his apparent position within the upper echelons of an intensely patriarchal society).

Once again, male anxiety is foregrounded and used as a narrative tool with which to reconfigure the concept of nationhood and national sentiment so that they both remain a by-product of an inherently masculinised culture. As a consequence, the representation of women in the film is significantly marginalised and acts as nothing more than a mere appendage of the anxious male gaze, both symbolically and visually (there are several subjective shots that mirror Dong-Sik's personal viewpoint). Female identity, depth and dimensionality are therefore diminished and, more problematically, the image of the Korean woman is rendered as hyperbolic and false. While it is entirely possible to argue that presenting different versions of female identity within the domestic space is progressive, the women in *The Housemaid* have little emotional autonomy. They are not portrayed as independent or complex beings. Instead, all the female characters remain conditioned by several exterior factors—primarily the expectations of genre (notably film noir and the melodrama), narrative and social/national ideology.

Above all else, the women of *The Housemaid* are, to a large extent, habituated and controlled by the relationship they share with Dong-Sik, known also as the 'Husband/Father' (which is also, no doubt, an allusion to the rigid familial systems implemented by Confucianism). They also serve specific and oppositional functions within the narrative. The 'wife' acts as the dutiful, almost silent, domestic partner—a reflection of Confucian sensibilities and a figurative constant to be protected. She also wears traditional Korean clothing: a white 'hanbok' that offers a stark juxtaposition to the darkened interiors in which the film takes place. The housemaid, meanwhile, whose black, Westernised attire grows increasingly form-fitting as the film progresses, acts as the unpredictable, destructive and promiscuous counterpart—a force that threatens to destabilise the hierarchical relations embedded within a middle-class, nuclear unit.

While the latter character is an erratic figure with an almost labyrinthine psychology (and, again, acts as an extension and/or result of patriarchal anxiety), her exaggerated presentation is used to merely reinforce the expected structures of traditional marital relations. When the character becomes a 'dangerous threat', as Kyung Hyun Kim continues, she 'must be eliminated in order for familial stability to be restored', which implies that the act of transgression, in the instance of *The Housemaid*, is applied only to the female figure (Kim 2004, p. 241). Sexual misdemeanours within the domestic space remain fundamentally gendered. In spite of the husband's apparent infidelity, he is still presented as a clear victim and, again, a figure for whom we are supposed to feel sympathy. Therefore, after a series of events which threaten to destroy not only Dong-Sik but also his entire family, it is above all the housemaid who must first suffer and ultimately die.

By the narrative conclusion, domestic equilibrium and, subsequently, patriarchal order are re-established. Regardless of the revolutionary presentation, the ideology of the time persists. While some would argue that Dong-Sik also suffers punishment and demonstrates repentance, it is the death of the housemaid, the supposed antagonist, that remains the greatest narrative priority. The film makes it clear that as a spectator, whether male or female, our concern, interest and empathy should be directed at Dong-Sik alone. When the film was first released in 1960, this desired response was achieved and, more interestingly, it was the female audience members who were openly 'hostile', demonstrating a clear hatred for the housemaid (Kim 2004). Evidently, Dong-Sik's influence, as a character, a man and, controversially, an embodiment of national/patriarchal identity, extended far beyond the cinema screen.

Crucially, this demonstrates a pivotal connection between the male protagonist, the diegetic world he occupies and the spectator's comprehension of certain narrative events. In *The Housemaid*, there is the continued sense that the space, the landscape, the women, the story and, perhaps, the audience are controlled by Dong-Sik or, at least, act as a symbolic augmentation of his interior psyche. Here, the concept of ownership is further solidified in the concluding moments of the film, when he speaks directly to the camera, effectively commenting on the world that he himself has created, and secures his relationship with the viewer in a highly conspiratorial manner. It is, indeed, this very nature of male ownership (and its connection to the wider construction of nationhood) that has often, though not always, problematised South Korean cinema's engagement with female identity and, more importantly, presented women on screen as nothing more than vessels designed to help or hinder the transcendental journey of the male protagonist.

This formula also links specifically to the conventional paradigms of film noir, which is arguably a genre that endeavours to 'other' the female presence and privilege masculine narration, despite its subjectivity and thus, unreliability. Dong-Sik's final address to the camera somewhat solidifies the generic parameters of the film with regard to its construction of the relationship between gender, genre and narrative (though not in relation to form and style, which remain highly experimental for the time). There is an obvious connection between the way in which Korean 'maleness' is presented on screen and the familiar structures embedded within commercialised/recognisable film discourse. Ultimately, *The Housemaid* incorporates the more common aspects of film noir (particularly those associated with the presentation of gender) to further localise its own narrative. It takes a genre that is already symbolic of patriarchal anxiety and transforms it into a Korean parable, using the destabilising figure of the housemaid in particular, or the 'femme fatale', to warn of the encroaching West and the potential loss of long-standing, hierarchical Confucianism (which contributes to a fragile masculine consciousness in traditional Korean society). Therefore, the depiction of female characters in the film remains greatly informed by both generic and ideological expectation. The wife and the housemaid are moulded by textual and cultural obligation and ultimately, they must serve a specific function in order to occupy any credible and conclusive space within the story—however fleeting it may be.

I would argue that this gendered formula has been repeated throughout the development and eventual rise of South Korean cinema. The profound influence of *The Housemaid* (and in particular its rendering of female characters as functional, transparent and practical narrative 'components') extends far into the new wave period and beyond. Whether it be the sacrificial 'pansori' singer, Song-Hwa, in the historical melodrama *Sopyeonje* (1993), the superficial and saccharine love interest, Jina, in the socially and politically charged *Chilsu and Mansu* (1988) or, more recently, the ambiguous figure of Mi-do in the neo-noir thriller *Oldboy* (2003), the expendable woman has remained consistent across genres and narratives within South Korean film (because she is a product of a national, commercial and patriarchal industry). On occasion, these female characters may have power, influence and importance within the broader story, as is evidenced by the destructive powers embedded within the titular character of *The Housemaid*, but they often remain trapped or narratively bound by their obligation to either serve or sabotage a male counterpart. Even the popular 'hostess' films of the 1970s typically ended with 'a heroine sacrificing herself for the sake of a man, a family and/or the nation', as Molly Hyo Kim observes—which, again, posits a symbiotic relationship between nationhood and masculinity (Kim 2014, p. 455). Clearly, this discourse is not bound to a specific point in history—it reappears in many different forms and guises.

Collectively, this demonstrates how the engagement with clear genre paradigms, alongside the subsequent consolidation of a specifically cultural narrative (achieved via generic experimentation), still pose a significant disservice to the representation of Korean female identity on screen. Arguably, this issue occupies a greater, more visible space in contemporary South Korean texts, which often function in a more transparent way with regard to genre discourse (albeit initially). As South Korean cinema becomes more commercially aware, it is more likely to draw attention to certain generic frameworks, modes of genre and thus, masculinised narratives. We can therefore begin to identify an exclusive trend of 'clustering' Korean texts that are male-oriented, highly marketable, internationally aware when considering style and form, but at the same time, nationally specific with unique Korean inflections. However, the presentation or consideration of Korean female identity is rarely treated as an integral part of this ostensibly successful, commercial blueprint.

Im Kwon Taek's *Sopyeonje*, for example, is particularly problematic with regards to its presentation of the sacrificial and expendable female character. The events of the film are delivered in a non-linear style, following the life of adoptive son Dong-Ho as he reflects on his childhood and adolescence, remembering his travels with his strict father, Yu-Bong, and sister, Song-Hwa. Their livelihoods depend entirely on the performance of 'Pansori' (traditional Korean music), and the film follows their journey across an evolving and modernising Korea. Similarly to *The Housemaid*, the film is considered, retrospectively, to be a major national achievement. It emerged in the midst of a 'culturally barren landscape' and helped to revitalise the growing domestic film industry during the early 1990s (Cho 2002). Certainly, one cannot dispute the film's importance and wider social impact. Its strong focus on 'Pansori' allowed domestic audiences to re-engage with and celebrate their own history, heritage and culture— aspects of national identity that, for many years, had been threatened or stifled completely by numerous exterior forces.

Nevertheless, this positive outlook and response cannot be similarly applied to the film's construction of gender roles and, in particular, its debatable presentation of the main female protagonist, Song-Hwa, who 'is depicted as if she were were born only for Pansori, never feeling hunger or, despite her youth, sexual or romantic urges', as Cho Hae Joang observes (Cho 2002, p. 145). Essentially, the character is deprived of her humanity and rendered as nothing more than a cultural and historical symbol—a voiceless and, at times, vacuous, narrative device used to mitigate the often tense relationship between her father and brother. For the majority of the film, Song-Hwa is trapped between two dominating pillars of oppositional Korean masculinity and, by extension, two opposing versions of Korea itself. While her father yearns for the past and devotes his time entirely to the preservation of 'Pansori', her brother recognises the inevitability of change and the social transformations that are taking place across the landscape. Even though the narrative draws attention to a crucial, generational divide here and symbolises the conflicted emotions experienced by a nation undergoing systemic periods of development and social reconstruction, it remains explicitly linked to the lived experiences of men. As a result, the greater and more pressing issues of nation, identity and Korean national consciousness are connected solely to the male characters and the masculine psyche.

Song-Hwa, meanwhile, stands on the periphery, oscillating between her father and brother, who continually use her as a tool with which to heighten their own sense of self-righteousness and patriarchal power. Despite her role as the primary 'Pansori' performer (and a figure with whom the spectator can use to form a nostalgic connection to the Korean past), the way in which Song-Hwa is manifested on screen significantly diminishes her narrative importance. This is perhaps most evident during the concluding moments of the film, which are often considered to be the most controversial. When, as Kyung Hyun Kim observes, Yu-Bong's 'overzealous ambitions to protect the national art against foreign cultures ... translates into an act that blinds his daughter', Song-Hwa's sacrificial role and greater purpose is definitively realised (Kim 2011, p. 243). More problematic than the act itself, however, is the lack of criticism imposed on Yu-Bong afterwards by both the narrative and other characters. He is not punished for his actions and eventually dies with his dutiful daughter by his side, who remains physically and emotionally wounded by her father's endeavours. Upon a narrative shift to the present (the early 1960s), Song-Hwa, now an adult, continues to perform 'Pansori' and awaits the return of her brother. Unlike the moving, transforming and changing South Korean landscape (which must negotiate the encroaching presence and overall growth of the urban, modern and global spheres), she has remained static—a constant and unmoving fixture of both the narrative and the national history it endeavours to celebrate.

This character outcome would not be as unsettling were it not for the continued influence of Yu-Bong and Dong-Ho, who continue to exert a spiritual control over Song-Hwa even when they are not physically present on screen. Ultimately, the character is trapped not by history or, indeed, by her obligation to perform 'Pansori'. She is instead burdened by the ubiquitous and unyielding expectations of a family and a society that are deeply patriarchal. Even though the film attempts to justify Song-Hwa's conclusion by suggesting that her greater cultural service is an entirely self-determined pursuit, the continued presence of masculine authority undermines her independence and, more importantly, calls into question the emotional legitimacy of her actions. Similarly to *The Housemaid*, a sense of male ownership permeates the narrative and threatens to manipulate our own response to certain characters and situations.

Unlike *The Housemaid*, however, where certain representational decisions can be considered as a direct reflection of Confucian ideologies and an extension of a conservative time period, *Sopyeonje's* questionable approach to gender cannot be similarly validated by the rigid constraints of history (despite being partially set in the early Twentieth century). The film was, after all, released in the early 1990s when long-awaited social changes were taking place across South Korea—namely the spread of democracy and the initiation of the economic 'boom'. As such, one might assume that the social transformations taking place across the landscape would also, to some extent, manifest themselves within popular entertainment—especially in South Korean cinema. Problematic depictions of female identity, however, have remained fairly consistent, even as other aspects of South Korean film have dramatically developed (when regarding approaches to genre and narrative, subversive discourse and commercial awareness, etc.). Even though there are always exceptions to this trend, and progress, in terms of both textual and commercial practice, has certainly been made, there still appears to be an absence of conscientious motion and movement with regard to the representation of Korean women on screen. The questionable portrait of female identity in Korean cinema, past and present, continues to tarnish what is otherwise a largely successful, and nationally aware, industry.

New Beginnings: The Revival of Gender Heterogeneity

New perspectives are often needed to initiate some form of change. In this instance, working *women* directors in the Korean film industry have, understandably, identified the long-standing trend of the expendable and/or destructive female protagonist in Korean cinema, but rather than pursue its demise (a largely improbable outcome), they have instead sought to question its continued popularity and challenge its origins. If, for example, we completely condemn the stringent approaches to gender roles displayed in a film like *The Housemaid*, we fail to fully comprehend the impact of the social, cultural and ideological landscape of South Korea in the 1960s. As previously mentioned, we must always acknowledge the broader systems and structures that create these distinctive and, at times, difficult stories and situations. Fundamentally, *The Housemaid* and, indeed, *Sopyeonje* remain important historical artefacts and should always be considered as such. Despite problematic approaches to gender presentation, their wider impact within the domestic film industry and their interest in specific national issues cannot be overlooked or forgotten. Therefore, the main issue to consider here is how and why similar gendered perspectives still occupy a prominent space in the post-millennial era, not only within film but in all areas of Korean popular entertainment. Whether it is due to the ambivalent desires of contemporary audiences, a masculinised film industry, the continued influence of traditional Confucianism or, indeed, the persistence of patriarchal thought in wider Korean society, there is the sense that these themes will never completely dematerialise. Thus, a focus on the new has become the preoccupation of women working in film. Difference is key to progress and there is now a shared desire to create a fresh narrative—one that is sustained, structured and informed entirely by female identity, voice and experience.

There are many reasons why Jeong Jae-Eun's *Take Care of My Cat* should be regarded as a pivotal South Korean text. It not only challenges the dominant narratives of Korean patriarchy, but it also (from the perspectives of industry and film practice) blatantly refuses to engage with the prevailing cinematic modes of the contemporary period. The film follows the everyday trials and tribulations of five young women as they attempt to navigate their lives after high school graduation. From this description alone, *Take Care of My Cat* can initially be regarded as a realist text (at least when compared to the other films discussed within this book). There is no spectacular event around which the narrative revolves, nor is there any dramatic shift in genre and pace. As Chi-Yun Shin maintains, the 'emphasis is on character rather than story' and is therefore in 'direct contrast to the energetic, goal-driven extravaganzas of the *jopok* genre'—a term used to describe the popularity of the post-millennial Korean gangster text (Shin 2005, p. 129).

Indeed, the film is a technical, thematic and stylistic outlier when considering the development and commercial agenda of the Korean national film industry at the turn of the Twenty-first century, which may go some way as to explaining its initial failure at the box office. During this time, South Korean culture was beginning to solidify its place on the global stage, particularly with its cinematic endeavours and popular music. Collectively, domestic media from this period manifested a specific image of Korean society—an image of economic prosperity, transnational awareness, urban progress and hyper-modernity (all of which have contributed to the nation's soft power). The city of Seoul has also been instrumental to this process and, more importantly, to South Korean cinema's engagement with genre and commercial film discourse. Popular Korean films released at the turn of the Twenty-first century, such as the aforementioned gangster text, the romantic comedy or the Korean blockbuster, often support the spectacular image of urban excess. They contribute to a specific, yet masculinised, national effort—to show South Korea (and Seoul specifically) as a fundamentally desirable and dynamic place, far removed (in some instances) from its own traumatic history and formerly vulnerable state. *Take Care of My Cat*, on the other hand, dismisses this overarching narrative.

This does not necessarily mean that the film and its creator are criticising the 'jopok movies' associated with this particular era of filmmaking, nor does the refusal to engage with certain cinematic paradigms make the text 'less Korean' or nationally specific. On the contrary, *Take Care of My Cat* remains an observational and reflective piece, providing a momentary snapshot of post-millennial female adulthood, its place within an evolving Korean society and, more significantly, a transitional (and sometimes conflicted) national consciousness. It has 'many of the characteristics of an art-house film … in its introspective quality and concern with the mundane', as Chi-Yu Shin continues; thus, 'it is not easily identifiable in terms of genre' (Shin 2005, p. 119). In light of this, it is important to note that while *Take Care of My Cat* bears some resemblance to an art-house text (largely for its observational style), it cannot and should not be labelled as such.

Despite being known for its occasionally abstract and subversive qualities, art cinema is still classed as a definitive, recognisable film category and must therefore operate, to a certain extent, like a commercial genre. We have, for example, a certain set of pre-conceived expectations when watching an art-house film, which suggests that, as a genre, it is susceptible to the same kind of standardisation as the thriller, the horror or even the romantic comedy. Even though it has already been established that genre does not possess the same structural rigidity in contemporary South Korean cinema, particularly within the films of Bong Joon-ho (as a more obvious and popular example), one has to acknowledge that in order for something to be defamiliarised, it is assumed that it must first engage, in some capacity, with the familiar. Bong Joon-Ho's works are, indeed, subversive, but they still acknowledge the standard conventions embedded within genre discourse.

Take Care of My Cat does not do this, and this is largely because of its female-oriented narrative and female director. There is the sense that in order for the film to truly break away from the formerly and formally dominant, masculinised aesthetic, it must completely abandon the commercial parameters introduced and sustained by a patriarchal film industry. This largely entails a new approach to story, tone and visual style. From the beginning, it becomes immediately evident that the film evades any and all categorical frameworks, be it through character construction, the absence of narrative causality or the manifestation of a distinctly 'unspectacular' landscape (albeit one that is still specifically Korean). While it does, on occasion, demonstrate the idiosyncrasies associated with art cinema or even the 'buddy movie' as Chi-Yun Shin also maintains, it never fully commits to a singular generic path or, indeed, a hybrid one (Shin 2005, p. 117).

One might also argue that *Take Care of My Cat* knowingly occupies the liminal spaces *between* genres and, as a result, fluctuates between a commercial and independent style. The suggestions of conventional film discourse are certainly evident, but they are removed or abandoned *before* properly permeating the tone of the film or finding any substantial place within its narrative. As such, the film demands an entirely different and, more importantly, *new* approach from its audience. Often, we can rationalise the emotional trajectory of a certain character or better understand the movement of narrative when the generic parameters of a film are made plain from the beginning. Fundamentally, genre informs expectation (or so the rules and long-lasting influence of studio-era Hollywood would have us believe). Therefore, when genre discourse is not only subverted but taken away altogether, such expectations are rendered useless.

As a result, it becomes increasingly difficult to decipher what exactly *Take Care of My Cat* sets out to achieve or communicate as a film text. However, this may be the primary aim of the film: to show rather than tell and thus give a certain amount of control back to the spectator (which, as has been previously established, goes against the masculinised narratives of more commercially viable, cinematic fare). Evidently, there is no greater agenda or immediate message in *Take Care of My Cat*, just a desire to reexamine what constitutes the familiar and, by extension, draw attention to the masculinised ideologies that regularly condition, shape and influence both popular South Korean cinema and the national film industry. More importantly, there is a complete lack of the aforementioned (male) 'ownership' in *Take Care of My Cat*, particularly with regard to the position of the audience and, above all else, the presentation of, and the response to, certain characters.

In terms of its form and narrative approach, contemporary South Korean cinema is widely characterised by its strong level of hybridity and its ability to seamlessly blend, interweave and ultimately subvert different tones and styles. Whether this hybridity can be applied to the presentation of gender, however, remains ambivalent (especially when considering the construction of female characters in typically male-dominated narratives). *Take Care of My Cat* quickly recognises this representational flaw and seeks to rectify the issue by creating a story-world that focuses solely on the female voice. Alongside the five main characters, all of whom are women, there is a continued sense of diversity and difference with regard to personal conditions, aspirations, desires, relationships and backgrounds. It is also worth noting that not all these characters are always likeable, admirable or, in fact, relatable. Some of their actions remain questionable and open to criticism. It is important to recognise, however, that this criticism does not stem from male anxiety (as it may have done in the past). It is instead a reflection of character complexity. The negative attributes that some protagonists display in *Take Care of My Cat* are both personal and linked to the specific lived experiences of women (both universally and in the Korean context). They are not necessarily a product of patriarchal unease or a tool with which to project masculinised concerns.

This is not to say that men, or the presence of a patriarchal expectations, are entirely absent from the film. Masculine influence is portrayed both positively and negatively (which, again, highlights the film's desire to establish gender heterogeneity). Crucially, however, this influence remains on the diegetic periphery—a quiet force that sways, yet never fully conditions or dictates, the movement of the female characters. This approach is, no doubt, a reflection of Jeong Jae-Eun's desire, as both director and writer, to showcase and fairly focalise the female voice (but not, necessarily, to the detriment of the few male characters that also exist within the story-world). Every shot of the film is conditioned by the experiences of women—women in the workplace or as part of a family unit, facing the daily pressures of urban life and the expectations of an increasingly globalised society. This is a rare accomplishment, particularly within a national cinema that has been measured and, to some extent, tainted by either problematic portrayals of women on screen or, more controversially, an absence of women altogether.

GOODBYE TO 'SEOUL': QUESTIONING URBAN PARADIGMS AND READING NATIONAL IDENTITY AS MYTH

As a means of further differentiating its female-centric narrative, *Take Care of My Cat* begins in a place that is, notably, *outside* of Seoul's intensely urbanised centre (thus, the film is immediately rejecting certain paradigms associated with Korean film discourse). The main characters live in Incheon, a heavily industrialised port city. As Chi-Yun Shin observes, 'a connection can be forged between the girls' outsider/marginalised status and Incheon' given its situation on the 'outskirts' of the capital city, which is considered to be the centre of culture, society and opportunity (Shin 2005, p. 129). For both domestic and international audiences alike, Incheon is arguably an unfamiliar, though not entirely alien, cinematic landscape. Even at this early stage, the film is seeking to explore and ultimately redefine representational norms by *not* utilising the same diegetic patterns found within other South Korean films released during the immediate post-millennial period (namely the standardisation of Seoul as a primary filmic landscape).

Incheon, while still clearly a city, does not function in the same way as the larger and substantially more developed capital. Nor does it engage with the broader idea, purpose and concept of the cinematic metropolis (something that also relies on the construction of, or clear engagement with, genre discourse). Whether this is an intentional decision on the part of the filmmaker is something that perhaps remains ambiguous, though one might argue it primarily operates as a way of further disconnecting the main characters from the ubiquitous presence of the capital city and, by extension, the wider image of a modernising, globalising and seemingly progressive South Korea. Ultimately, *Take Care of My Cat* endeavours to dissolve the touristic portrait of the country (something that has been continually facilitated by the masculine experience, narrative and/or male gaze) and, in particular, the dynamic and mythologised illusion of urban space or urban existence.

By living in a city that initially seems different from the capital, all five female characters are presented as socially and economically disadvantaged. They are also intensely isolated. More importantly, there is the suggestion that the circumstances of Hae-Joo, Tae-Hee, Ji-Young and twin sisters, Bi-Ryu and Ohn-Jo, are conditioned not only by their geographical and national placement but also by their gender. As Yaeri Kim observes, the five (female) characters often 'desire and dream of alternative lives and selves in a society that disenfranchises them in different ways' (Kim 2015, p. 150). Unlike, for example, the Korean gangster genre, in which male on male violence is both served and celebrated by the city (and the hypermodern society it manifests), or the 'monster-epic', in which the familiarity of Seoul champions ordinary male heroism, the urban landscapes in *Take Care of My Cat* offer no such praise, liberation or spectacle. They only create further challenges and obstacles for the characters, particularly in the primary setting of Incheon, which is often presented as an urban repository of missed opportunity, unemployment and stagnant livelihoods (more so for young women than men).

This is not to say that the capital is entirely absent from the film, nor is it presented in a positive way (i.e. in stylistic and symbolic opposition to Incheon). On the contrary, it features significantly in Hae-Joo's personal storyline, as she must make the daily commute there in order to further her career prospects. Even though the visual transition from one city to another forms the opening credit sequence, the film does not exaggerate the differences between Incheon and Seoul as clearly as one would initially expect. Hae-Joo's home residence is situated in a poverty-stricken neighbourhood riddled with crime. The bleak landscape is awash with grey, blue and black. A coldness permeates the diegesis, casting a melancholic shadow across every building, down every street and through every windowpane.

Clearly, this is not a land of hope or opportunity. It is a space frozen in time and a place from which Hae-Joo must temporarily leave in order to improve her financial status, social reputation, independence and subsequent happiness (or so she believes).

When she arrives in the capital, however, it is immediately apparent that *Take Care of My Cat* is not committing to the same, ubiquitous and enterprising image of Seoul as its commercialised counterparts. Instead, it is portrayed as an impersonal and hyper-modern space—a city that, in some ways, is losing its own history and identity. The streets abound with high-rise buildings and suit-clad residents, emphasising Seoul's function as a working realm (though not, necessarily, a place that is easily accessible to all). As previously discussed, one must take into account the year in which the film was released, the exponential growth of the national film industry at the time and the subsequent investment in the big-budget, South Korean blockbuster (which relies heavily on a spectacularised image of the cityscape), to fully understand this visual dismissal of the 'norm'. Evidently, *Take Care of My Cat's* pragmatic and, perhaps, cynical engagement with urban space presents a strong stylistic divergence not only from the patterns inaugurated within the (male-dominated) Korean film industry but also from the long-established relationship between cinema and the metropolis. The film does not celebrate the celluloid city. It instead questions the previous presentations of cinematic urban space (particularly in South Korean film), effectively rendering such portraits as false and hyperbolic.

Therefore, a focus on the 'real' is of paramount importance. Shot entirely on location, *Take Care of My Cat* engages with cinematic urban space in a highly unfamiliar way, by completely stripping away its filmic and imaginative properties. In this instance, one must also consider the role of director Jeong Jae-Eun, who is predominantly known for her short films and, most significantly, documentary filmmaking. As a result, the observational stance of the camera in *Take Care of My Cat* evokes a naturalistic gaze, positioning the spectator in a world that appears authentic and far less celluloid. At the same time, however, one must recognise that this presentation is explicitly linked to the subjective experiences of all five female protagonists. This is *their* reality—a subjective world that, in many ways, remains burdened by the masculinised Korean landscapes of the past and, indeed, the present.

Kim Bora's *House of Hummingbird* (2018), a much more recent cinematic text, presents Seoul and the wider Korean social landscape in a similar way. The film follows Eun-Hee, a conflicted and frustrated teenager living in a working-class Seoul suburb. Throughout the film, the character must learn to navigate the various personal obstacles of adolescence—all of which are set against the backdrop of 1990s South Korea and a time of continued social and economic change. Eun-Hee's family home is indicative, as Tomris Laffly observes, of the Korean capital's 'undisciplined real estate expansion', and this detail is specific to the era in which the film is set (Laffly 2019). From a global and broad historical perspective, we tend to think of this time period in South Korea as a phase of substantial economic and cultural growth. While this is, to a large extent, true, *House of Hummingbird* focuses on the identities that exist *outside* of this prevailing narrative. In the opening moments of the film, Eun-Hee is seen returning to her residence after a short trip to the grocery store. She initially rings the wrong doorbell, having confused her own doorway entrance with another. When she eventually returns to the correct residence, the door closes and the camera zooms out, revealing rows upon rows of identical apartments, on numerous different floors. Evidently, rapid urban developments have somehow compromised the social, cultural and historical autonomy (and perhaps integrity) of the city and its residents. Eun-Hee, meanwhile, is clearly monopolised by the transformations and changing infrastructure of her insular world—a world from which she can neither escape nor truly belong within. Like the characters in *Take Care of My Cat*, Eun-Hee similarly embodies a separateness. She often inhabits the disparate spaces of the diegesis, which further emphasises both her physical and emotional isolation. The interior spaces of the film also highlight this separateness. Eun-Hee's homes act as a microcosm of the wider patriarchal systems and structures that are felt and experienced across South Korean society. Her position within the household is clearly dependent on, and limited by, her gender. She is regularly abused by her older brother, who often receives preferential treatment from her parents—and this favouritism is presented as an unconscious, normalised *bias*. Even her own room is located far from the other 'lived' spaces of the apartment, illuminating not only a clear gender divide but also a generational one.

It isn't until Eun-Hee is introduced to her new female Chinese language teacher, Miss Kim, that her personal narrative begins to change. Upon the entry of this pivotal character, the restrictive and masculinised spaces that formerly conditioned Eun-Hee's existence start to transform (which demonstrates the power of female friendship). As a result, she begins to see beyond the borders of her immediate realm. Her classroom, especially, becomes a kind of sanctuary, and she starts to engage with her surroundings in a new way, taking an interest in books on politics, democracy, feminism and culture. Fundamentally, Eun-Hee's interactions with Miss Kim allow her to evaluate her own identity (or whatever 'identity' may mean in this context), in order to rise above the expectations of the space, family, society and nation in which she is placed.

A focus on the 'other' therefore, or in this case, that which is not ostensibly 'Korean' in nature, proves to be an intriguing concept within both *House of Hummingbird* and *Take Care of My Cat*. In the latter text, transnational pursuits and globalised ambitions are key components of the narrative. While the characters clearly remain comforted by the familiarity of South Korea, there is a strong, collective belief that hope, success and opportunity lie elsewhere, far beyond the geographical border. This is particularly significant when considering Incheon's placement and function as a port city, which, ironically, relies on movement, travel and a sustained connection to the outside world. The characters' physical proximity to escape is apparent, yet they remain inextricably bound to the landscape, trapped by the shared responsibility to support their families and restricted by their poor socioeconomic status. Evidently, this conflict between duty and desire becomes a source of tension between the protagonists as the film progresses, particularly when Hae Joo reminds Ji Young that 'going abroad' is an unlikely prospect, given that she has no money (primarily because she must take care of her elderly grandparents). In this instance, one might argue that Incheon also acts as a perpetual reminder of family (and, symbolically, national history and heritage) and is therefore a place to which all the characters feel obligated to return and ultimately stay.

Many conversations between the women take place by the waterside—a backdrop of freedom, openness and potential adventure. As previously mentioned, movement is a key aspect of the film. Whether by bus, train or simply on foot, every character has, ostensibly, the opportunity to travel across the filmic landscape, but this does not necessarily mean they can or, in fact, will. Throughout the film, there are also several shots of the moving diegetic space: a traffic jam in Seoul, the view through a bus window, a busy train platform and the eventual glow of city lights when dusk arrives. Interspersed throughout these shots are the Korean workforce— billboards showing women in suits, rows of market stall vendors and industrial labourers. There is a frenetic energy to the space; it remains a busy and modernising landscape. While this is clearly a world in constant motion, however, the five main characters remain in a static state: unmoving and stationary. The shots which take place inside buses particularly emphasise this sense of immobility, because the 'outside' world (which lies beyond the windowpane) contrasts with the stillness of the interior space and the frustrated protagonist positioned within it. Essentially, there is a distance between the five women and the 'lived' spaces of the diegesis. Thus, the concept and visualisation of movement within the film becomes a false promise—a desire that can never be made into a reality (at least not within the confines of South Korea). All the women are presented as transient beings, physically and emotionally trapped in a society from which they can neither leave nor truly stay within. They have no fixed 'place' within the diegetic world and as such, rely on the globalised, hyper-modern and progressive images and narratives they see and hear of to inform their personal aspirations and goals (even if these images are also, to some extent, constructed).

The film also articulates time in a highly distinctive way. When all five women are out together on a day trip, there are moments when it is hard to distinguish whether the film is in slow motion or if the characters themselves are moving at a different speed to their surroundings. The suggestion is that during the rare occasions when all the women are in one shot, the story-world temporarily loses its linearity, progress and tempo, thus highlighting the 'separateness' of the protagonists. Here, the film itself is attempting to provide a space, however fleeting, in which all the women can return to their former selves. Echoes of the past and, in particular, the positive atmosphere inaugurated within the introductory scene resurface. The present reality is momentarily forgotten and a strong sense of nostalgia overrides the narrative, particularly when the diegetic soundtrack begins and the dialogue is reduced to an absolute minimum. Nevertheless, these moments of reflection and meditative temporality are merely used to emphasise the cyclical existence of the characters who, despite undergoing and experiencing superficial changes, have arguably made little progress with regard to their personal or professional lives.

Therefore, the temptation to escape is palpable, particularly for Ji-Young, who wants to study abroad and 'sees a foreign country as a site of transformation that is impossible within the borders of her homeland', as Yaeri Kim observes (2015, p. 150). When considering the position of women in contemporary urban society, the film establishes an oppositional portrait of East and West here. Despite its modernising exterior, the former is rendered as a conservative and suppressive realm, perpetually bound to a gendered past and its underlying, yet persistent, engagement with traditional Confucianism—long-lasting and deeply embedded structures that still occupy a significant space in society. The latter, meanwhile, though never visited by the characters or physically presented on screen, is regarded as a contemporary utopia largely because it represents some form of *difference*. It is not necessarily a better, more attractive or, indeed, more progressive landscape (as is acknowledged within the film). It is instead perceived, by the characters, as a place entirely separate from the homeland and therefore, to some imaginative degree, desirable. The longing for this 'other' can also be seen in Eun-Hee of *House of Hummingbird*, who throughout the film begins to challenge that which is perceived as 'normal'. Whether questioning the hierarchical structures embedded within her family life or exploring a non-heteronormative romantic relationship, Eun-Hee demonstrates a will and desire to break out of the ideologically constructed, 'grand' narrative that surrounds her.

In light of this, I would argue that both films deftly call into question the formation of identity and its relationship with nationhood. Even though the self and the state are often presented as having a symbiotic connection (as seen in the texts discussed in the previous chapters of this book), *Take Care of My Cat* and *House of Hummingbird* seek to undermine and ultimately eradicate such ties. In the former instance, the character of Ji-Young believes that her own identity cannot, and should not, be defined by her responsibilities to serve a greater national and/or cultural purpose (particularly when the society from which she hails has already failed her in numerous ways). Even the close proximity of Seoul is not enough to entice her. This is in strong contrast to contemporary male-oriented narratives which, as we have established, seek to reposition the male figure as a functional, adaptable and evolving fixture of South Korean national identity—especially so within the gangster text. Fundamentally, such narratives explore themes of place and belonging. The complex journey of the male protagonist often represents Korea's equally complex history (thus positing nationhood and the masculine subject as synonymous, interdependent concepts). Therefore, finding one's place, identity and purpose is of primary concern in Korean cinematic narratives where issues of patriarchy and the patriarchal subject (of which there are many) are concerned. This pursuit is easy to realise on screen when considering how Korea's history is continuously read in terms of its relationship with the male subject and the shared masculine psyche. However, the position and personal stories of women within this now mythologised, national narrative have, up until fairly recently, remained on the outer perimeters of public consciousness. One need to only look at the neglected and overlooked experiences of Korean women during the Japanese occupation to fully understand the extent to which female voices have been excluded from the ostensibly collective, 'nation-building' endeavours of Korean society, from the long and complex Twentieth century to the present day.

In its own and, arguably, indirect way, *Take Care of My Cat* addresses this concept of constructed history and, by extension, the perceived values linked to the formation of a national identity (which, as we have now established, exists as symbolic expansion of an antiquated, gendered discourse). Yoon-Kyung Kwak argues that a 'sense of belonging, out of shared blood and ancestry, has played a pivotal role in allowing Korea to maintain its pride [throughout its turbulent history]' (Kwak 2018, p. 1192). For Korean women, however, who have been expected to 'maintain traditional and patriarchal cultural norms', this notion of belonging remains somewhat elusive (Kwak 2018, p. 1193). These expectations are addressed in both *House of Hummingbird* and *Take Care of My Cat*, and as such, the main characters must acknowledge the difficulty of locating their own, innate sense of 'Korean-ness', which inevitably leads to questions and anxieties regarding what exactly constitutes the 'Korean self' (in terms of female identity, place and space). Unlike their male counterparts, the women in these stories have no 'grand narrative' or 'history' on which to build their own identity—that is when 'history' refers to a version of the past that remains inherently patriarchal and therefore, on some level, mythologised. Without this central connection to historical narrative, the women arguably have no attachment to a *present* sense of nationhood, which may explain their resentment of, and feelings of disillusionment towards, contemporary Korean society.

Collectively, these character dilemmas significantly complicate previous approaches to, and definitions of, 'nation', 'national identity' and, to some extent, 'national history' (at least, when considered alongside female identity). Of course, it's entirely possible to argue that this issue isn't necessarily specific to South Korea. One might also argue that the obstacles the characters face in both films reflect the universal experiences of women in a hyper-modern, globalising urban environment and can therefore be read on an international spectrum. Nevertheless, while this may attest to *Take Care of My Cat's* and *House of Hummingbird's* accessibility (in terms of their commentary on female experience), it in no way undermines the cultural, social and national relevance or particularity of both texts.

Indeed, *Take Care of My Cat* (as an earlier and arguably formative text in Korean women's cinema) is particularly relevant in this discussion. Fundamentally, the film focuses on a highly specific South Korean landscape and its impact on five marginalised identities—a landscape that cannot be easily exchanged for any other. More importantly, the film's evaluation of nationhood as a concept, alongside its analysis of the masculinised attitudes that dominate Korean national consciousness, effectively draws attention to a flawed, historical system and structure. By addressing the negative subject matter born from nationalistic myth, I would suggest that, in many ways, *Take Care of My Cat* is more 'Korean' than the previous texts discussed within this book because it recognises South Korea's social or cultural issues and refuses to rectify them with idealistic solutions. Be it through narrative content, textual style or the unique presentation of the cityscape, the film focuses on the 'grey' areas that, together, form a more realistic portrait of national identity in the contemporary period. Above all else, *Take Care of My Cat* seeks to neutralise and modify the rigid ties between history and nationhood in order to create new space for the previously underrepresented—namely women.

A Different Kind of Girlhood? Reevaluating the Functionality and Relevance of 'Sonyeo' Narratives in Korean Cinema

The concept of girlhood has featured heavily in the wider narratives associated with East Asian Cinema, across many different genres and particularly so within Japanese film. In Korean cinema, however, tales of female adolescence have emerged as integral and, to a large degree, exclusive components of the contemporary horror narrative (Choi 2009). While this might be considered a problematic trend, as there is the dangerous potential for 'girls' narratives' to become codified within a solitary and sensationalised genre, it more importantly helps to manifest the necessary cinematic scope in which to explore previously marginalised issues. Jinhee Choi notes that films such as *Whispering Corridors* (1998) and *A Tale of Two Sisters* (2003) demonstrate how Korean teen horror 'grants a place for representing and expressing adolescent female sensibility, which hitherto has been neglected by many [other] mainstream genres' (Choi 2009, p. 56). Fundamentally, it seems that any exploration of female sensibility on screen is better than none at all, even when it is presented within, or functions as part of, a seemingly recognisable discourse.

How, therefore, might the concept of Korean girlhood operate *outside* of genre, when familiar filmic tropes cannot be used as tools with which to address specific cultural narratives (and, as a result, be subverted)? Essentially, *Take Care of My Cat* cannot perform in the same way as *Whispering Corridors* or *A Tale of Two Sisters* because it clearly works in opposition to commercial models and popular narrative discourse. It has already been established that the film does not engage with any one genre in a transparent way—it works far beyond any generic style or ascertainable framework. As such, *Take Care of My Cat's* relationship with 'sonyeo' sensibility is intentionally short-lived. The nostalgic opening sequence illuminates the fleeting and bittersweet nature of Korean girlhood by focusing on a momentary 'snap-shot' of school life. It is, in fact, the only time in the film when we see the women as teenagers. Thus, by offering no expositional narration before or after this scene, we are denied a clear, coherent or conclusive picture of girlhood.

In one respect, this may act as a form of criticism, by showing (in a manner that is highly self-aware) how Korean culture and society has continued to peripheralise, or erase entirely, the stories of female adolescence throughout popular entertainment and a patriarchal society. From another, and perhaps more controversial, perspective, the scene is used to challenge the approaches to girlhood displayed in previous texts like *Whispering Corridors*, where a reliance on genre paradigms has arguably resulted in hyperbolic and inflated representations of young, female identity (and takes place within landscapes that are overtly dramatised). Even though these representations are, indeed, relevant and important, they must, in some capacity, remain controlled by the boundaries, 'rules' and conventionalities of the horror-world in which they are conceived—and also by the expectations of the audiences who help to sustain it.

In contrast, the minimalist and naturalistic portrait of girlhood in *Take Care of My Cat*, however brief it may be, shows how narratives of female adolescence need not be conditioned by genre (and, by extension, the ubiquitous presumptions of the spectator). Girlhood cannot, and should not, be trivialised or embellished with the extraneous details that, collectively, contribute to the 'make-up' of a specific cinematic discourse. While the Korean teen horror text can, by all means, be recognised as a sustainable outlet for depicting 'sonyeo sensibilities', one must acknowledge the extent to which its engagement with a definitive textual mode complicates narrative representation. Of course, the clear counter-argument here, as Jinhee Choi notes, is that the portrayal of 'sonyeo sensibility' is capable of transforming the 'generic norms of the horror genre', which will thus challenge pre-conceived expectations and possibly create a more nationalised or localised product in the process (Choi 2009, p. 47). While this is certainly true and can also be applied to many other genres (given South Korean cinema's capabilities of breaking down representational norms), it is still important to question why narratives of girlhood are contained within, and are therefore disciplined or refined by, a specific cinematic mode. As *Take Care of My Cat* demonstrates, authentic representation of female identity can unfold in the liminal spaces *between* genres, separate (or at the very least partially disconnected) from the concrete realms of popular cinematic structures—as well as the patriarchal institutions in which these structures are created and maintained.

As previously mentioned, *Take Care of My Cat* takes this theory a step further by deliberately withholding certain information from the audience, which therefore renders girlhood as a transitory, though by no means inconsequential, experience. A sense of rebellion, both textually and narratively, is apparent throughout the opening sequence. The scene is too short to form any immediate connection to genre, has little temporal or spatial coherence and, as a result, denies the spectator a definitive moment in which to manifest a lasting and potentially limiting impression of the overall text. Our perception of the diegetic world is entirely reliant upon the female characters, who not only control what we see on screen but also our response to it. This may have not been possible had the genre of the film (and thus, the stylistic and thematic parameters of the narrative) been made clear from the beginning. The manner in which the interaction between the girls is captured further emphasises their unparalleled ownership of the space or landscape and, more importantly, their own identities. As they celebrate the end of their final day as high school students, they take pictures of each other along Incheon's port-side, accompanied by the sound of incoming barges and ferries. The sun is setting, which acts as a fitting reminder that a significant period of time is coming to a conclusion. The girls' interactions are followed and replicated by the camera, which shakes, jolts and sways with the same delight and anticipation. The specific approach to cinematography is especially significant in this moment. Rather than observing the events on screen from a stationary distance, which allows the audience to form an objective judgement of events, the camera moves alongside the characters, replicating their frenetic energy.

As a consequence, the spectator is momentarily immersed within the action and included in the group. In fact, the entire opening works to immediately abolish the inherent objectivity of the celluloid world and instead create something far more personal, intimate and, ostensibly, real.

Nevertheless, while there is a sense of collective joy and excitement for what is to come in this moment, *Take Care of My Cat* quickly and self-consciously abandons this idyllic image of Korean girlhood (a portrait entirely of its own design) in a manner that questions whether it is ever possible to capture 'sonyeo sensibility' accurately and honestly on screen. In retrospect, the opening scene functions as a hazy and romanticised homage to what used to be. It is merely an affectionate glance at the past. Soon after, the film turns to the present day and to what appears to be a far darker and colder landscape. The contrast between these two settings not only signifies, on a more practical level, a passage of time, but it also demonstrates a dramatic shift in the physical and emotional state of the characters and their potential agency in the landscape. As a result, girlhood is swiftly taken away from the protagonists, from the film itself and from us. One wonders whether it ever existed in the first place. Even the conclusion of the introductory sequence is marked by a dissolve/fade, as though it has been extracted from a dream. Thus, what was once a 'real' event now seems entirely imaginary—especially when the bleak and austere landscape of present-day Incheon fills the screen. Indeed, the use of the landscape is critical here, as the diminishment of girlhood is paralleled by a diminishing vision of the city and what it seemingly represents: hope.

To at once manifest, celebrate and ultimately relinquish such an emphatic and vivid depiction of Korean girlhood demonstrates how *Take Care of My Cat* operates as a critical, national and, above all else, female-oriented text. It aims to draw attention to the experiences of Korean women without necessarily providing a concrete or conclusive idea of what exactly constitutes Korean female identity. In this respect, *Take Care of My Cat* succeeds where so many other texts have failed, because it acknowledges the complexities, inconsistencies and innate heteroglossia of its primary subject. Be it girlhood or womanhood, the film remains aware of the personal and private nature of specific concepts linked to the formation of female identity and therefore refuses to provide a complete and comprehensive picture on which the spectator, or the narrative itself, can pass judgement. Only by stepping away from genre, interpretation, dramatisation and, most importantly, social speculation can this be achieved.

Conclusion

Take Care of My Cat is no ordinary film. Nor can it be considered as an ordinary Korean text. As the popularity of South Korean cinema grows, and the industry's national, formal and thematic characteristics become more defined and potentially commercialised, *Take Care of My Cat* will prove to be a necessary, historical outlier. This is, indeed, a rare feat when considering the already subversive and experimental nature of South Korean cinema as a whole. Yet, Jeong Jae-Eun's directorial debut manages to evade all expectations and, in doing so, contributes to the industry's reputation as an inimitable, autonomous and nationally aware institution. While the film exists on the periphery of Korean popular culture, it remains securely woven in the fabric of the country's national cinematic consciousness. This is because it speaks directly to those who are marginalised without necessarily chastising the wider systems and structures that have, collectively, contributed to the development of Korean society in the post-millennial era. It essentially satisfies two different, yet entirely equal, national narratives. Most importantly, the film offers a crucial take on a subject that has previously been overlooked: the fragile nature of female friendship and its impact on female identity. Even amidst personal hardship, conflict and struggle, a persistent, yet subdued, sense of sisterhood binds the characters together throughout the majority of the *Take Care of My Cat*. The titular cat is a key signifier of this connection, as well as a 'fitting symbol for the vulnerability and resilience of the young women', as Chi-Yun Shin observes (2005, p. 128). 'Titi', as the cat is affectionately known, sustains the relationship between the women even when they themselves have neither the time nor the desire to see one another.

During the moments in which relations are strained, it is often implied, through the use of sound and editing, that the metropolis is acting as a peripheral presence, constantly threatening to destroy the sisterhood and all that it represents. On several occasions, the urban environment literally overwhelms the voices, bodies and identities of each protagonist, compromising their very existence within the diegesis. This is significantly different to the opening sequence, which effectively places the characters at the heart and centre of the filmic world, albeit very briefly. The celluloid metropolis is repeatedly filled with disturbances and unwelcome interruptions, especially when the relationships between the characters are at their most vulnerable—strained by obligations to their families or, more critically, to one another. In one pivotal argument that takes place between

Hae Joo and Ji Young, and latterly between Hae Joo and Tae Hee, the sounds of the surrounding cityscape prove to be an intrusive presence. In one instance, the women stand on a busy train platform, quarrelling over their present commitments. As their feud escalates, so too does the sound of an approaching train. All the integral facets of the narrative at this point are reaching a technical and symbolic crescendo. While the dialogue is sometimes difficult to decipher, the intent is clear, especially when Tae Hee eventually decides to board the train. Her departure is significant in this moment, as there is the sense that she is not only leaving what was once a close friendship behind, but she is also criticising and rejecting the livelihood that Hae Joo has so readily accepted (and with it a 'version' of female identity that has been sustained by the expectations of a largely male-oriented society).

As a result of the fall out with Hae Joo, the bond between Tae Hee and Ji-Young grows stronger, primarily because their interests, wishes and aspirations are similar. Their friendship is solidified in the concluding scene of the film, when escape and the possibility of dreams turning into a reality are finally realised (albeit only partially). The sequence takes place at Incheon airport, a space that has been visited several times throughout the film but, up until this particular moment, has never fulfilled its true purpose. As both characters stare at the departure board, with a plethora of possible destinations to visit, there is the feeling that the present reality of the filmic world is shifting. Notably, we cannot see either of their faces in this moment (a notable difference to the opening scene, where the girls' faces occupy the majority of the frame, often in close-up). The effective anonymity of the characters here is used to inaugurate a sense of the 'new'—new identities, new choices and new landscapes.

However, the point of the final scene is not to show what the characters are moving towards. It is instead a celebration of the fact they can move at all. In this concluding moment, Tae Hee and Ji-Young have the freedom to say 'good bye' to South Korea (whether it be temporarily or long-term). Crucially, their departure is never fully realised on screen, primarily because their ultimate destination is of little consequence. More importantly, there is little to indicate that they will remain forever separate from their home country. After all, the film is not so idealistic as to suggest that the characters' problems will be solved in another country, culture or society. It merely attempts to show how transnational pursuits often inform the idea of the 'other' or, in this instance, that which cannot be realised, achieved or even truly 'seen' within the homeland. In response to the readings of Karen Lee Kelsky, Yaeri Kim analyses this notion of collective female yearning and concludes that a 'longing for the foreign can be seen as a symptom that reveals the failure of a local society' (2015, p. 151).

Ultimately, *Take Care of My Cat* concerns itself with these revelations and asks why such 'longings' exist—particularly within Korean women. Instead of looking elsewhere for answers or seeking a solution to these aspirations, the narrative focuses on 'transnational fantasies', by 'tracing the trajectories of the desires and imaginations rather than actual movements'—hence why, in the end, we never actually see the characters in any other national setting (Kim 2015, p. 151). The film does not, at any point, intend to show where Tae Hee and Ji Young will go, nor does it divulge their future selves to the spectator. On the contrary, it seeks to understand why its characters, like so many other Korean women, wish to leave their homeland in the first place.

References

Cho, H. 2002. Sopyeonje: Its Cultural and Historical Meaning. In *Im Kwon Taek: The Making of a National Cinema*, ed. David E. James and Kyung Hyun Kim, 134–156. Detroit, Michigan: Wayne State University Press.

Choi, J. 2009. A Cinema of Girlhood: Sonyeo Sensibility and the Decorative Impulse in Korean Horror Cinema. In *Horror to the Extreme: Changing Boundaries in Asian Cinema*, ed. Jinhee Choi and Mitsuyo Wada-Marciano, 39–56. Hong Kong: Hong Kong University Press.

Gitzen, T. 2013. Affective Resistance: Objects of Korean Popular Music. *International Journals of Asia-Pacific Studies* 9 (1): 5–36.

Howard, R., and B. Brian Yecies. 2015. Korean Cinema's Female Writers-Directors and the "Hegemony of Men". *Gender a Vyzkum* 16 (1): 14–22. https://doi.org/10.13060/12130028.2015.16.1.167.

Kim, K. 2004. *The Remasculinization of Korean Cinema*. Durham: Durham University Press.

———. 2011. The Transnational Constitution of Im Kwon-Taek's Minjok Cinema. *The Journal of Korean Studies* 16 (2): 231–248. https://doi.org/10.1353/jks.2011.0018.

Kim, M. 2014. Genre Conventions of South Korean Hostess films (1974–1982): Prostitutes and the Discourse of Female Sacrifice. *Acta Koreana* 17 (1): 455–477. https://doi.org/10.18399/acta.2014.17.1.017.

Kim, Y. 2015. Desiring Displacement: Globalisation, Nationalism and Gendered desires in 'Take Care of My Cat'. *Journal of Japanese and Korean Cinema* 7 (2): 149–166. https://doi.org/10.1080/17564905.2015.1087153.

Kwak, Y. 2018. Pushing Away from Their Own Nation? South Korean Women Married to Migrant Husbands from Developing Countries. *Ethnic and Racial Studies* 42 (7): 1186–1203. https://doi.org/10.1080/01419870.2018.1473620.

Laffly, T. 2019. House of Hummingbird Review. *Variety*. Accessed 10 September 2021.https://variety.com/2019/film/reviews/house-of-hummingbird-review-1203199577/.

Paquet, D. 2017. The (few) Women Breaking Through in Korean Cinema. *BFI*. Accessed 26 March 2020. https://www.bfi.org.uk/news-opinion/sight-sound-magazine/features/women-korean-cinema.

Seong, T. 2003. 9 Lives? 'Cat' Lovers Just Want 2. *Korea JoongAng Daily*. Accessed 17 February 2020. https://archive.is/20120710013056/http://koreajoongangdaily.joinsmsn.com/news/article/article.aspx?aid=1896963.

Shin, C. 2005. Two of a Kind: Gender and Friendship in 'Friend' and 'Take Care of My Cat'. In *New Korean Cinema*, ed. Chi-Yun Shin and Julian Stringer, 117–131. Edinburgh: Edinburgh University Press.

CHAPTER 6

The Oppositional City

In 2017, following its debut at the Cannes Film Festival (where it also competed for the coveted Palme D'or prize), Bong Joon Ho's *Okja* was released on the worldwide streaming platform, Netflix. Given the director's growing profile and the continued international popularity of South Korean cinema (and of Korean popular culture more generally), this seemed like an appropriate step. Digital accessibility is, after all, key to success in the media/entertainment industry and as the 'worldwide appetite for Korean cultural content' grows, so too do the ways in which this content can be consumed and shared amongst a global audience (Kim 2011, p. 1). Marketed as a promising Korean/American co-production with a majority English-speaking cast (though it is still, notably, categorised as a Korean/foreign language text), the film follows Mija, a young girl who lives in the outer mountainous area of Seoul, in a forest, alongside her 'super pig' Okja. The gargantuan creature is the result of an American breeding programme and, as we later find out, an experimental response to the global demand for mass food production. When Okja is eventually taken by the company that created her, the 'Mirando Corporation', Mija and her supposed allies must work together to retrieve the animal.

The films of Bong Joon Ho have already received a substantial amount of attention thus far within this book, and one can clearly identify the stylistic patterns that have remained consistent across the director's broad catalogue of work (particularly with regard to his idiosyncratic approach to tone, genre and narrative). *Okja*, however, stands somewhat as a formal anomaly. From a comparative perspective, the film does not sit as easily or, indeed, as comfortably alongside its predecessors, which may be due to the overt 'Americanisation' of its narrative, characters and settings. Notably, however, *Okja* does not mark director Bong's first exploration of international, collaborative film practice. This title is reserved for *Snowpiercer*, a film that arrived significantly earlier, in 2013, and was shot primarily in English. The story, adapted from a dystopian French graphic novel, takes place almost entirely inside the expansive 'Snowpiercer' train, which carries the last of humanity on a cyclical, global track. When the poor and neglected passengers (who are situated at the back of the train) decide to rebel and fight against the aristocratic elite (who occupy the front of the train), a narrative of class-warfare ensues. As Julian Stringer and Nikki J.Y. Lee note, Bong's adaptation 'internationalises its characters by having them speak in a range of languages' and also notably includes two Korean protagonists: a father and a daughter (Lee and Stringer 2017, p. 269). The film features a range of different identities and the insular, isolated world in which it takes place acts as a microcosm of a globalised, multi-cultural and multi-ethnic society. Therefore, *Snowpiercer's* narrative concerns itself with the international. It is *not*, by definition, a South Korean text (because it doesn't engage with or reflect a predominantly Korean landscape). Fundamentally, *Snowpiercer* is a commercial film that addresses the global community (even as it demonstrates certain Korean inflections or 'Bongisms' within its stylistic approach and/or the overall production). As a result, we have a clearer idea of how to respond to the film and its overarching message. The transnational blueprint of *Snowpiercer* heightens the overall accessibility of the text, which is absolutely crucial for a narrative that concerns and seeks to comprehend global identities and, more significantly, illuminates oppositional class structures.

Nevertheless, the same cannot be said in relation to *Okja*, which, unlike *Snowpiercer*, has a significant portion of its narrative set in South Korea. As such, it is assumed that the film must, to some extent, engage with certain Korean issues, perspectives and national paradigms. Initially, *Okja* seems to do this and successfully so (which is why it has been continuously marketed as a Korean/foreign language text). Nevertheless, as the narrative progresses and other, non-Korean elements are introduced, the national specificity of the text inevitably dematerialises. As will soon be made clear, the greater issue here is how the integration of another landscape (in this case America and, more specifically, the city of New York) eventually problematises the supposed 'Koreanness' established at the beginning of the text, displayed within the infant stages of the story. The comparative aspects of the narrative (East vs West), complicate certain representations of cultural, social and historical space and, as a result, undermine *Okja's* position as a national text—even with the support of a prolific South Korean director. This is particularly significant when taking into account Bong Joon Ho's current status as a recognisable Korean auteur and, above all else, the manner in which his works have, collectively, contributed to a nationally aware and culturally unique, cinematic landscape and aesthetic. Notably, *Okja* has not received the same kind of attention as *Memories of Murder* (2003), *The Host* (2006) and *Mother* (2009), nor has it be given the same level of academic scrutiny with regard to its ostensible relationship with national cinema or its impact on the domestic film industry in South Korea. As a result, one must inevitably analyse the film's position and place on Bong's directorial timeline and, by extension, question its relevance in the wider realm of commercialised, post-millennial South Korean cinema.

To what extent *Okja* operates as a successful Korean text, or even as a piece of clear genre filmmaking, remains fairly ambiguous, especially when considering the defining characteristics linked to the concept of national cinema (which, in its simplest form, concerns films that reflect a particular nation state). A sense of 'separateness' pervades both the narrative of the film and its production, despite a clear engagement with specific Korean landscapes and a narrative which largely focuses on the journey of a Korean protagonist. Furthermore, while *Okja* engages with many of the expected components associated with a 'Bong Joon Ho production' and, on a more general level, demonstrates some of the subversive qualities linked to contemporary Korean cinema, it cannot properly establish or consolidate its own identity. Ultimately, *Okja* is a conflicted text, largely because it oscillates between different styles, alternative modes of cinematic discourse and, most importantly, contradictory narrative goals. While this approach may, to some extent, evoke the 'Korean style' (largely because it fosters a sense of unpredictability and, latterly, challenges generic expectations), it is not used as a device to localise the narrative. And as I have established thus far within the previous chapters of this book, the South Korean film industry's ability to nationalise the paradigmatic approaches to popular cinema is paramount to sustaining its position and reputation as an autonomous, culturally unique institution.

Given that *Okja* is partially produced by an American company, incorporates an American narrative with American characters and settings, and was released, initially, by a leading American media platform, one must expect an inevitable diminishment of Korean sensibility within the overall text. It is also important to recognise for whom the film is ultimately intended and as such, one might argue that *Okja* seeks to privilege and satisfy the expectations of an international audience as opposed to a domestic one. The issue, therefore, is not necessarily the text itself but the manner in which the audience is expected to respond to it and/or interpret the story. The insistence of its own 'Korean-ness', even with the aforementioned Americanisms, places *Okja* in a problematic and indefinable space (particularly if we consider its ostensible relationship with both national cinema and the now recognisable characteristics of Bong Joon Ho's directorial style).

Above all else, however, *Okja* may be indicative of how the Korean film industry intends to diversify in the future—primarily through the conflation of different modes of film practice and production. If this be the case, what might the conceptual and structural ramifications be for national cinema as both a theoretical framework and a process through which we can better understand different film cultures? While it is no exaggeration to say that all national, cinematic landscapes are influenced by wider, global approaches (whether in industry or practice), observing and defining a nation's unique approach to filmmaking is a process to be maintained. This is now more important than ever, particularly in the age of rapid globalisation. If, however, *Okja* functions as a small indication of the transnational ambitions of not only the South Korean film industry but also many other film industries around the world, the future of national cinema (which here refers to the act of recognising films that reflect, engage with or represent a particular nation state) may be put in serious jeopardy. As stated previously, this concern is not designed to undermine or criticise the creative value of cross-global film collaboration and production. On the contrary, I wish to highlight how, alongside this development, we must continue to take a national approach to understanding world cinemas in order to better isolate the cultural specificities and individual societies they represent. Thus, the process of nationalisation, in the context of film studies, need not be necessarily viewed as an archaic or problematic concept. It can be used as a tool to highlight the overall heteroglossia and diversity that remains deeply embedded within the international film landscape.

Adversarial Cities: Utopian and Dystopian Representations of Urban Space

The global narrative of *Okja* is established within the first few moments of the film. It opens with a commercial for the 'Mirando Corporation', as the titular CEO herself, Lucy Mirando, speaks directly to the camera and to us, the spectator. This 'glitzy and flamboyant press release', as Dennis Wilson Wise notes, should 'instantly raise red flags for the audience', particularly when it is succeeded by a shot of an 'idyllic and isolated mountain reserve in South Korea' (Wise 2019, p. 291). Even at this early stage, the film is laying down the foundations upon which the oppositional, diegetic landscapes of the narrative are built and sustained. Evidently, the world of *Okja* revolves around a clear set of binaries: namely East vs West, Korea vs America and, latterly, Seoul vs New York. The audience is expected to automatically accept these binaries and the manufactured, national perspectives they create.

Of course, antithetical representations of the East and West have been used before and, in terms of South Korean cinema, can be used to successfully localise a once broad, cinematic narrative (as such perspectives often provide a space in which to explore the country's complex, national history). In this instance, however, the immediate depiction of two confrontational settings is used to foreground and emphasise the marked disparity between two cultures and two collective, social identities. Mija and Okja's 'isolated mountaintop home' is like a fairy-tale and 'offers what global capitalism cannot: stability, predictability and containment', as Ju Young Jin notes (Jin 2019, p. 5). However, while it may appear entirely separate from the bustling city of Seoul, it is soon revealed that Mija's residence is more closely situated to the capital city than is initially made apparent. One would expect, given the connotations and assumptions linked to urban space, that Seoul's close position to Mija's home is designed to present a symbolic threat—namely the looming presence of modernity, expansion and globalisation.

However, it soon becomes clear that this is not the case (and thus demonstrates the film's immediate rejection of specific urban stereotypes when considered alongside a Korean landscape). *Okja* often characterises Seoul by its close proximity to, and strong relationship with, the natural environment. Sweeping long shots present the city as a harmonic extension of the forest—different, but by no means out of place or juxtapositional. Lush, dense greenery surrounds the urban landscape and gradually merges with the roads, avenues and minor passages that lead towards the centre of the metropolis. Ultimately, everything within the diegesis appears interconnected and, more importantly, the urban and natural world are entirely compatible. Flashes of green remain ever-present, trespassing in and out of the frame. Trees and flowers are growing in the every-day, lived spaces of the city, alongside the undulating roads of Seoul's suburban perimeters. Even the post-production colouring seems intentionally naturalistic.

Mija's frantic movement across the landscape also reveals the various levels, layers and characteristic structural imbalances that have, collectively, shaped the development of the city. The streets and buildings exist as physical and symbolic extensions of the mountainous, hilly and rugged land on which they were built. As such, a sense of history constantly penetrates the architectural plains of the space, which emphasises the temporal hybridity of the overall landscape and the many different identities and voices that exist within it. There is a utopian quality to the city, as though everything exists in harmonic balance, and this allows the 'small town/the pastoral' to exist alongside and within 'the age of globalisation', as Ju Young Jin continues (Jin 2019, p. 2).

However, one must acknowledge the extent to which this particular depiction remains far removed from the touristic picture of the capital, which is firmly entrenched, like many other globalising cities, in the idea of excess, progress and consumerism. This broader picture is deliberately avoided in *Okja*, as it would compromise the narrative direction of the film and, latterly, complicate the emphatic comparisons made between Seoul and New York. Therefore, the spatial limitations of the urban landscape are made plain from the beginning. In many ways, the presentation of Seoul in *Okja* evades the contemporary (in the sense that the globalised spaces and heteroglossic sub-structures of the city are not fully realised on screen). This is not to say that the film completely evades the more intensely urbanised zones of the metropolis (at one point, Mija is dwarfed by a group of suit-clad businessmen when emerging from the subway, for example), but it is consciously presenting Seoul as a landscape that is sympathetic and responsive to the natural environment—and not, therefore, like other developing cities. Ultimately, the depiction of Seoul in *Okja* is bound by narrative obligation and, as a result, diverges from the representations of Korean urban space addressed previously in this book. While films such as *3-Iron* and *Take Care of My Cat* (or even the other works of Bong Joon Ho) portray the city as a hybridised landscape, filled with a diverse mixture of old and new spaces, *Okja* provides only a limited view of the city and its residents. The intensely urbanised centre of Seoul is never fully explored or present on screen, despite the fact that both the audience and the characters know it exists. The suggestion of 'something more' is certainly apparent—evidenced by fleeting glimpses of sky-scrapers, traffic jams and ominous concrete fixtures—but it remains elusive and never compromises the constructed serenity of Mija's immediate realm.

Nevertheless, as the film progresses, it becomes clear that the distinctive presentation of both Seoul and its surrounding landscape serve a specific purpose, primarily because a second, and ostensibly different, metropolis is also interrogated. During the latter half of the film, we enter New York City—or what might be considered as an intensely hyperbolic version of it. Here, the streets and buildings are direct extensions of the American characters we encounter throughout the narrative: artificial and outlandish, with highly saturated appearances and overtly performative exteriors. New York is likewise presented as a heavily manufactured and heavily stylised space, devoid of authenticity and, indeed, any concrete sense of reality. The buildings often frame the screen, acting as concrete borders that overwhelm and obstruct the diegesis. Rather than enhance the contemporary nature of the space, they overpower it completely, hindering its accessibility to both the spectator and the characters. It is an impenetrable prospect, especially for Mija, who, in her quest to find Okja, is persistently overwhelmed by this foreign world and the dominating characters with whom she comes into contact. As Mark Kermode observes, her 'diminutive frame … [contrasts] starkly with the giant structures of the cities in which she ventures' (Kermode 2017).

A performative façade constantly disturbs the landscape, which undermines the legitimacy and reliability of the 'American' narrative and its primary characters. Clearly, this is a city of many simulations—a vast repository of falsehood and fabrication. Above all else, however, this representation is used to further highlight the anti-American sentiment that is deeply embedded within the structural discourse of the film. Antipathy towards the West, whether direct or indirect, fluctuating or constant, has occupied a substantial space in South Korean cinema, especially so within the films of Bong Joon Ho. This is, no doubt, a reflection or extension of certain national attitudes and the movement of the national consciousness as a whole. Seung-Hwan Kim argues that from the millennial period onwards, 'Anti-American sentiments have now spread into almost all strata of Korean society' and are unlikely to dematerialise at any point in the future (Kim 2002, p. 109). As a means of further nationalising and localising its own narrative, *Okja* emphasises the criticism of the West on a more literal level by having its main character, a child, venture directly into it. Everything we see, therefore, is conditioned by Mija's subjective experience—an immediate impression of America as told by a formerly sheltered and innocent girl with little knowledge of the exterior or urban world.

This presentation is, of course, designed to manipulate the perspective of the audience and manifest a highly condemnatory image of the West. In this particular instance, America acts as the symbolic and physical antithesis of Korea—unnatural, hyper-modern and dangerous. Even though narrative antipathy towards the West is, as previously mentioned, not uncommon within South Korean cinema, it is particularly noticeable and, to a large degree, exaggerated in *Okja* (which is particularly problematic when considering its precarious relationship to the Hollywood style). Whereas Bong's previous works demonstrate criticism of the West via peripheral and secondary narrative strands (often as implied plot-points that, whilst understated, remain highly disparaging and accusatory in nature), the anti-American sentiment in *Okja* forms a substantial part of the narrative and remains a primary focus in the overall story-world. As soon as the American characters enter the Korean space, the potential narrative intricacies embedded within Mija's personal life, home, and world are quickly removed and as such, the cultural details of a national landscape are left unexplored. It therefore becomes difficult to decipher at what point the film might be considered a definitively 'Korean text', given that a predominantly Americanised landscape and narrative are introduced so early in the opening stages of the film.

Conflicted Sentiments: Attachment, Antipathy and the Urban West

Christina Klein argues that 'Bong's films embody an ambivalent relationship to Hollywood, and they bear the marks of the equally ambivalent relationship between South Korea and the United States', which may account for their hybrid and transnational nature (Klein 2008, p. 872). This has certainly proved true for many of Bong's films. However, in the case of *Okja*, the operative concept of 'ambivalence', with regard to both subject matter and style, cannot be as readily applied. The film follows a linear narrative and rarely 'mutates', 'bends' or challenges the expectations of the audience in the same experimental manner as films such as *The Host* and, more recently, *Parasite* do. Therefore, instead of defamiliarising the familiar or subverting generic discourse (thus highlighting the textual ambivalence to which Klein refers), *Okja* re-establishes certain modes of popular discourse and returns to the commercial realms of narrative causality, linearity and exposition. Any semblance of so-called ambivalence, therefore, grows increasingly difficult to identify, both in terms of film style and technique and the social sensibility of the story.

In Bong Joon Ho's previously discussed film *The Host* (2006), an American pathologist orders his Korean subordinate to dispose of chemical waste by pouring it down a drain, releasing it into, and ultimately polluting, the Han river (which is used as a clear and consistent national symbol within the film). Thus, it is implied that the resultant monster of the story is of American design—a by-product of the pathologist's carelessness and authoritative position. Even though the scene is brief and is used to merely explain the origins of the monster, it still functions as a reminder of Korea's historical, highly complex and, at times, tense relationship with America. Indeed, the distinctive presentation of the two families in Bong's most recent film, *Parasite*, is also indicative of this tension, though the film is arguably less critical than its predecessors (including *Okja*). However, *Parasite's* satirical approach draws even closer attention to the growing influence of the West in South Korea, essentially building on the same levels of unease and resentment. In one humorous scene, a wealthy Mother insists that her child eat his ramen with cubed steak mixed in, an expensive and unnecessary addition to a staple, Asian meal. It is this self-awareness and comedic self-reflexivity that has allowed South Korean cinema (and Bong Joon Ho's films specifically) to deftly negotiate the line between reverence and ridicule when engaging with the West. Anti-American sentiment penetrates such narratives, but more importantly, never compromises global accessibility. It is always implied and never explicit or truly tangible within the diegetic space. In *Okja*, however, these sentiments are rendered as opaque criticisms, bereft of social, cultural or philosophical nuance. The comparative approach of the film, particularly with regard to the construction of urban space, is used to challenge previous representations of America on screen (namely those inaugurated and sustained by Hollywood).

As the portrayal of New York City has become a ubiquitous and centralised feature throughout Hollywood film, *Okja's* presentation of the renowned metropolis is both subversive and unexpected. America is no longer rendered as the 'centre' of the world (and this is where the text's anti-American sentiment is perhaps most obvious). Instead, it stands on the geographical periphery—unfamiliar, alien and, perhaps, inferior. Therefore, by essentially 'othering' the American city, *Okja* is re-establishing Seoul as the primary urban space and as the centre of the filmic universe. In this particular instance, the film is questioning the previously oppositional relationship between the East and West, namely by drawing attention to the problematic and often derogatory perspectives that still exist in relation to antiquated terms such as 'the orient'. As such, certain stereotypes are repositioned. *Okja's* highly subjective narrative (in which our own experience of certain events is directly informed by Mija's personal journey) renders America as a dangerous, foreign and, most interestingly, uncivilised space. Here, however, 'uncivilised' refers to a society whereby technology has significantly compromised human interaction and removed any semblance of the natural world.

Seoul, meanwhile, is presented as a landscape that is considerably more authentic than its Western counterpart. Previously, the texts addressed in this book have engaged with the South Korean capital in a critical way, acknowledging both the negatives and positives of an evolving and progressive space. In this instance, however, the presentation of Seoul does not invite the same analytical response, largely because it is rendered as an entirely desirable, naturalistic and, to a certain extent, tranquil place. When we leave the forested area in which Mija, Okja and her father live, and enter the centre of the metropolis, there is still an organic and unrefined aesthetic to the landscape, as though the stability and serenity of nature have crossed the threshold into the 'everyday' zones of urban existence. When Okja and Mija are chased into an underground market and subway alongside the 'ALF' (the 'Animal Liberation Front'), reality is grounded by the cool-toned colours, subdued lighting and the curious glances of surrounding 'Seoulites'. The sequence is also shot in slow motion and accompanied by a contrapuntal soundtrack: John Denver's 'Annie's Song' (which is, ironically, an American country song). These technical decisions serve a crucial function. Time itself is suspended and, more importantly, the generic aspects of a typical chase scene are lost entirely. There is no sense of speed or urgency here, which effectively makes the violence (instigated by the American forces of the Mirando Corporation) more disturbing. The change in temporality also allows the spectator to observe the 'naturalism' of the space in which this chaos unfolds. All of which creates an element of magical realism. While Okja is clearly a fantastical creature, the city that surrounds her is very *real*—or, at least, that is how it should be perceived by the spectator.

This is clearly a functional and utilitarian space—a reflection of a working city. At certain points, even Okja seems to seamlessly blend into the setting (which acts, no doubt, as another visual reminder of Seoul's positive response to the natural and animal environment). Despite the apparent level of fantasy embedded within the narrative and within this particular chase sequence, a sense of normality is sustained and is often used, as previously mentioned, to pacify the fantastical presence of Okja. More importantly, the ordinary and, perhaps, mundane nature of the Korean landscape also functions as a means of further criticising the homogenous, artificial and, perhaps, static spaces that are eventually introduced when the characters enter America in the latter half of the film. Often, the camera works to illuminate the differences between New York and Seoul. When, for instance, Mija chases after Okja in Korea's capital, the entire sequence functions as a journey of transition—technically, thematically and symbolically. The spectator is transported *through* the landscape, not *across* it. From the outer, less affluent areas of Seoul, towards the perimeters of its modern and contemporary centre, the naturalism and ostensible authenticity of the Korean environment is made apparent in a short space of time. As the camera follows Mija, it travels along the streets, moving in harmony with the changing landscape. Every building is different and every road leads to a different area, drawing attention to the depth of frame and the intricate backdrop of the metropolis. Evidently, there are a variety of layers, identities and textures that exist within this urban zone. Nothing appears entirely straight, balanced or stationary, including the camera itself, which serves to eliminate the celluloid properties of the scene and the space in which it unfolds.

New York, on the other hand, is presented as a metaphorical archive of singular identities, hegemonic cultures and hyper-modern archetypes. Nature is also obsolete. Before the characters physically enter the Western space, the loss of the natural environment is foregrounded when Mija breaks into the Mirando Corporation's headquarters in Seoul. While attempting to speak to the receptionist, she crashes into a fake, indoor tree, and as it collapses, we see that its 'roots' are nothing more than a tangled mass of wires and electrical circuits. This image is indicative of the broader sense of cultural binaries that *Okja* endeavours to highlight: nature versus civilisation (and technology), socialist authenticity versus capitalist performativity and the balanced East versus the disordered West.

Even within the confines of a seemingly ordinary office, the presence of America (and its subsequent threat to Korea's natural heterogeneity) becomes apparent. Wherever there is a clear overlap between these two landscapes or societies, there is also the continued 'threat' of hybridisation or cultural assimilation. As perhaps one of the most controversial aspects of the narrative, *Okja* makes the unequivocal assertion that these two worlds cannot, and should not, co-exist, which is surprising when considering the transnational manner in which the film was made, distributed and later marketed.

American forces constantly threaten the safety of the urban Korean spaces explored within the film, albeit indirectly, as well as Mija's home in the forest. When Johnny Wilcox, a zoologist and once popular TV personality, arrives to observe Okja in her home, he disturbs the former sense of balance and peace that is intrinsic to the natural Korean environment. The technical aspects of the film also change upon his arrival, highlighting how the character compromises the cinematographic discourse previously established in the introduction (primarily during those moments that emphasise the close bond between Mija and Okja). A 'faux' documentarian-style gaze replaces long, romantic establishing shots and intimate close-ups, especially when Wilcox interviews Mija and her father. What was once a highly naturalistic landscape is now an artificial construction—a stage on which Wilcox and his own camera crew can manifest a persuasive, practical and performative space. During one moment of postmodern mirroring, Wilcox replicates Mija's affectionate interactions with her 'pet' by stroking Okja's head, making eye-to-eye contact and leaning against her body. In this instance, however, the action is presented in a far more perverse and sinister way, primarily because we are aware of the cameras that occupy the diegesis. There are frames within frames here, and it becomes increasingly difficult to distinguish one celluloid world from another. The spectator's focus is manipulated by the desires of these characters and their ulterior motives. Narratives of immorality remain hidden under a synthetic and factitious surface.

Wilcox himself remarks how being a television presenter means always having to be 'on', yet his willingness to adhere to this rule suggests he does not view it with any particular disdain. Once again, the anti-American sentiment is especially magnified here, particularly when Wilcox's hyperbolic and overbearing role so clearly eclipses the tranquillity of the indigenous landscape and, more significantly, exploits the Korean identities that exist there. Allusions to Korea's complex history and its fluctuating relationship with America are largely expressed through the cultural and social dissonance experienced between the protagonists. It is not a case of miscommunication, but rather the impact of one dominant and controlling voice or presence overwhelming another. Even when Mija encounters the 'ALF', who seemingly want to help her retrieve Okja, the disparity between two cultures is evident. Like Johnny Wilcox, they also use Okja to serve their own personal and political agendas. Historical feelings of anxiety, and the fear of national corruption from an exterior, Western world, begin to take hold of the narrative and thus exaggerate the sense of antipathy towards America. This is not to say, however, that the film approaches these darker issues in a typically melodramatic or overly serious manner. Characters such as Johnny Wilcox and Lucy Mirando are presented as childlike and petulant—they grow frustrated and aggressive when their 'image' is compromised. This leads to several humorous and satirical interactions with other protagonists, including Mija (who, despite her young age, is considerably more mature and grounded than her supposedly 'adult' counterparts).

Nevertheless, while these depictions heighten the overall comedic aspects of the text, the derogatory intent is still evident, as is the subsequent desire to place the Korean characters on a moral pedestal. Genre experimentation and subversive characterisation are used to further sustain social opposition and show the Korean world as fundamentally 'better'. They do not function as a means to nationalise the text (which is what we have now come to expect from South Korean cinema). Again, here we can see how a focus on the 'other', or a desire to show that which is not Korean, problematises the local identity of the film. Fundamentally, the filmic aspects that have lately emerged as key characteristics of South Korean national cinema begin to unravel and dematerialise in *Okja*'s oppositional, comparative and, above all else, competitive filmic world.

The Trouble with Difference: *Okja* and the Dilemma of National Cinema

For a film that we are supposed to regard as a predominantly Korean text, involving America in any capacity poses a significant issue, as it implicates the legitimacy of certain representations of Korean society and the Korean landscape. *Okja* clearly attempts to solidify clear differences between South Korea and America through distinctive and contrasting representations of urban space. As the contrast is so vivid and, at times, hyperbolic, the overall manifestation of both cities on screen may be regarded as a tendentious reading of different global positions. This presentation is in direct contrast to Bong's other films, including *Parasite*, which arguably engage with the West (and more specifically America) in a less obvious and direct way, so as not to take focus from the primary narrative focus—Korea, Korean society and issues of national identity. By completely engaging with, and exploring, another landscape, *Okja* loses its credibility as a piece of national cinema.

Fundamentally, Seoul is presented as the physical and symbolic antithesis of New York. One must therefore question whether these distinctions are part of a comparative exercise or a means of emphasising global binaries, as opposed to true depictions of national landscapes. It could be argued that in its attempts to establish its own identity, difference and 'Korean-ness', *Okja* reduces two cities (and, indeed, nations), into imagined, or fabricated, spaces. As Jung-Bong Choi maintains, this 'rudimentary' paradigm of 'identity/uniqueness' no longer works when nationalising film, as it fails to recognise filmic intertextuality and, above all else, the complex questions of cultural 'plurality and diversity' (Choi 2011, p. 181). By differentiating Seoul and New York in such an exaggerated and occasionally caricatural way, *Okja* cannot properly locate the Korean narrative it so desperately seeks to sustain. It is, to a large extent, preoccupied with matters of difference and otherness.

Of course, there is the argument to be made here that meaning can only be achieved through difference.[1] However, this may only be applicable to a singular discourse and/or space that is simultaneously 'self-comparable', multifaceted in nature or dichotomous (as opposed to two separate and polarising concepts). If, for example, *Okja's* narrative had remained entirely entrenched within the Korean landscape, locating meaning (via difference) may have been possible, largely because the intricacies of Korean national culture would not be mitigated or, alternatively, exaggerated by the threat of any exterior presence. Instead, the inclusion of an evidently artificial American setting not only diminishes the cultural value of the film, but it also compromises its overarching, narrative message.

This once again highlights the necessity of nationalising cinemas and the importance of sustaining a specific cultural and thematic approach—one that perhaps engages, initially, with a domestic audience.

[1] In reference to Ferdinand de Saussure's structuralist readings.

Arguably, the *transnational* approach to the making of *Okja* has prevented it from securing its own identity and thematic autonomy. Regardless of its attempts to establish a clear polarity between South Korea and America, there is the continued sense that *Okja* is a transferable and interchangeable text, with no clear social or, indeed, national origin to 'ground' its narrative, characters and overall style. This, of course, would not pose a significant issue, had the film not been heavily promoted as a 'Korean story' in a global context—accessible to a world audience but still inherently unique and recognisable within a certain cultural framework. While they are obviously present to some degree in *Okja*, the stylistic qualities that are now intrinsic to South Korean cinema (subversive genre bending, allusions to national history, the acknowledgement of a unique national landscape, etc.) are somewhat mitigated, or appear out of place entirely, due to an increasingly globalised narrative and a desire to present America as 'other'. These unique idiosyncrasies only work in a world that is entirely Korean in its presentation—a trend that is normally present in the majority of Bong Joon Ho's work.

Another narrative aspect that compromises the 'Korean-ness' of *Okja* is the conclusive, expositional and cathartic nature of the final sequence, which not only highlights the transnational desires of the text but also alleviates and problematises the overall message of the story. After confronting the Mirando Corporation, Mija and Okja successfully return home to Korea, along with a stolen (and subsequently rescued) baby pig. The final shot consists of this 'new' family, together again in the Korean forest—a portrait of harmonic equilibrium. The fantasy or fairy-tale that was initially established at the beginning of the film is once again restored, and with it, an idyllic and utopian image of Korea—a setting that, by this point, is far removed from the chaotic events and spaces explored previously in the story. At the same time, we are reminded that the Mirando Corporation continues to thrive in America. There is now, however, a clear distance between these two narratives and landscapes. In its simplest form, Korea represents sanctuary, safety and positive isolation. Meanwhile, America represents, as we have previously established, the opposite. Fundamentally, the binaries that are introduced in the opening sequence of the film are not only re-emphasised by the end but solidified within the narrative and, perhaps, in the minds of the audience too.

What then is the ultimate narrative purpose of Mija's journey or, indeed, the overriding message of the film itself? While her ultimate goal is realised (as she is eventually reunited with *Okja*), the spaces that Mija visits throughout the film do not undergo any form of transformation—including her own home. They continue to exist as static and enduring celluloid constructions. A desire for 'movement' or change, therefore, is left unfulfilled, despite the philosophical stance the film appears to take in the introduction. Ultimately, this neat resolution evokes the familiar style of popular/commercial discourse and, as a result, pushes *Okja* further away from its ostensible Korean roots. Indeed, one might argue that while the narrative endeavours to be anti-Hollywood, it still operates, as Jia Yin observes, within a 'Hollywood-type' system, mainly because its core messages are mitigated or diminished altogether by conventional structures and vague narrative approaches (Yin 2018, p. 61). This is where the conflicted messaging of the film is at its most apparent—not just within the narrative itself but also in the overall style and formal approach of the text.

Conclusion

The function of this chapter is not to criticise the transnational, collaborative endeavours of a Korean auteur but to show how a desire to address the 'global' can result in a conflicted and, occasionally, inauthentic depiction of a single nation. On a more practical level, *Okja* is also a text that allows us to form more concrete ideas about what does, and does not, constitute South Korean cinema. Ultimately, this chapter is designed to provide a point of contrast—to show how the 'transnational' (which, in this instance, concerns texts which address multiple landscapes) can be an overly fluid framework that risks diminishing important national paradigms. More significantly, *Okja's* visual difference, underwritten by its transnational production, devalues previous conceptions of Seoul, the city and, by extension, South Korean identity.

At one stage in the film, a pivotal conversation takes place between Mija and the members of the ALF, during which the Korean translations provided for Mija are deliberately (and comically) altered by an interpreter. As a result, the innocent character is given a modified and skewed version of the mission on which she is about to embark. In many ways, this minor scene is indicative of the miscommunication and conflicted messaging displayed in the broader narrative of the film itself. Be it in the narrative style, the formal aesthetics or even in the overall commercial approach, *Okja* stands as a confused film, a self-proclaimed Korean text that feverishly oscillates in and out of the popular spaces associated with the Hollywood style (even as it attempts to abandon or criticise such parallels). Therefore, like Mija, we as spectators are engulfed by a false narrative—the words and intent are clear, but the final 'translation' remains fundamentally flawed.

References

Choi, J. 2011. National Cinema: An Anachronistic Delirium? *The Journal of Korean Studies* 16 (2): 173–191. https://doi.org/10.1353/jks.2011.0012.

Jin, J. 2019. Making the Global Visible: Charting the Uneven Development go Global Monsters in Bong Joon-Ho's *Okja* and Nacho Vigalondo's *Colossal*. *CLC Web: Comparative Literature and Culture* 21 (7): 1–10. https://doi.org/10.7771/1481-4374.3659.

Kermode, M. 2017. Okja Review. *The Guardian*. Accessed 13 November 2019. https://www.theguardian.com/film/2017/jun/25/okja-bong-joon-ho-netflix-review-mark-kermode.

Kim, S. 2002. Anti-Americanism in Korea. *The Washington Quarterly* 26 (1): 109–122. https://doi.org/10.1162/016366003761036525.

Kim, K. 2011. *Virtual Hallyu: Korean Cinema of the Global Era*. Durham, N.C.: Duke University Press.

Klein, C. 2008. Why American Studies Needs to Think About Korean Cinema, or, Transnational Genres in the Films of Bong Joon Ho. *America Quarterly* 60 (4): 871–898. https://doi.org/10.1353/aq.0.0041.

Lee, N., and J. Stringer. 2017. *Snowpiercer*: Sound Designable Voices and the South Korean Global Film. In *Locating the Voice in Film: Critical Approaches and Global Practices*, ed. T. Whittaker and S. Wright, 263–278. New York: Oxford University Press.

Wise, D. 2019. Bong Joon Ho: 'Okja'. *Science Fiction Film and Television* 12 (2): 290–294.

Yin, J. 2018. Analyse the Narrative Mode of Bong Joon Ho's Films Through Okja. *Journal of The Korean Entertainment Industry Association* 12 (5): 61–67. https://doi.org/10.21184/jkeia.2018.7.12.5.61.

CHAPTER 7

Conclusion

In an article titled 'American Horror Story: How the US Lost its Grip on Pop Culture', Steve Rose cites Bong Joon Ho's *Parasite* as a key cinematic text that 'provided another jolt to US supremacy' and subsequently challenged America's position as a 'cultural gatekeeper' (Rose 2020). However, while the film has certainly helped to sustain, and perhaps solidify, a crucial power shift between Korea and America, this comparative approach still perpetuates many antiquated perspectives. The fact that *Parasite* is repeatedly compared to, or read within, the Americanised spaces of popular entertainment demonstrates the extent to which Western cultural output is still considered to be the benchmark against which all other national voices and creations are measured. Whether this approach will ever completely dematerialise is uncertain, but it is now highly necessary to recognise why such comparisons are problematic and, from a more troubling perspective, continue to position the East as oppositional 'other'. Steve Rose's article further highlights this approach, as it infers that the diminishment of US popular culture is responsible for the growing cultural production and success stories of other world industries. It is suggested that the growth of South Korean cultural output is dependent on the failure of its American counterpart. This is, of course, a questionable approach, as it fails to acknowledge the self-determined development, scale, appeal and power of the South Korean cultural landscape.

Ultimately, the need to define the South Korean film industry in terms of its relationship with, or connection to, Hollywood cinema is quickly becoming a counterproductive exercise, as is the more inherent practice of comparing and contrasting Korea's cinematic endeavours with those of other East Asian nations. While its history and development may remain inextricably tied to these exterior voices and identities (a national matter that is often addressed in its own cinematic endeavours), the future of the South Korean film industry is becoming ever more self-determined and self-governed. Whether the US is losing its cultural dominance is no longer an issue or, indeed, a serious variable to be considered, largely because the Korean entertainment industry now has the materials at its disposal to forge and sustain its *own* success as a national institution. It does not need to rely on the failings of other national industries to either boost its development or increase its accessibility (particularly on a domestic scale), as significant investment by the localised government means that funding from exterior sources is not always needed. Jeongsuk Joo elaborates on this, noting how the 'dramatic changes in the Korean film industry cannot be adequately grasped without looking at the role of the Korean government' (Joo 2010, p. 152). Collectively, the changes to both the cultural landscape and the growth of cultural production in the country have been the result of a shared, nationalised effort and a localised desire to invigorate South Korea's post-authoritarian image—and perhaps step away from (though by no means forget) the collective trauma that has continually defined and shaped its national narrative.

Of course, this tremendous level of success and progress has not gone unnoticed by other international industries. Therefore, it is now important to not only recognise the South Korean film industry as an autonomous, localised institution but also acknowledge its increasing global influence. Recently, it was announced that *Parasite* would be adapted and/or expanded into a limited television series for the American network HBO, possibly featuring an American cast alongside some of the original Korean cast members from the film (Ruiz 2020). This may prove to be another example of the *Okja* syndrome. As the popularity of South Korean cinema and South Korean popular culture grows, Hollywood is more likely to take an interest in the country's national productions, especially those with narratives that have the ostensible potential to be 'Americanised'. Remakes and adaptations are, it seems, inevitable (though, as we have previously established, this is not always an easy or rewarding process). Regardless of how Hollywood intends to alter, adjust or modulate Korean cinematic narratives in the future, it will never be able to truly replicate the thematic visions of a text such as *Parasite*, because these visions remain deeply specific to a South Korean, national discourse. However, the fact that Hollywood is looking to incorporate or assimilate any exterior narrative into its own commercial blueprint is a testament to Korean cinema's growing international dominance in aspects of both production and practice.

Seoul, be it as an image, concept or 'real' space, has been instrumental to this growth and to the global projection of South Korea as a desirable and culturally rich landscape. It features across all cinematic genres (culminating in the subsequent 'Seoul genre' and a sustained focus on the celluloid metropolis), narratives and discourses, providing a template on which to create and sustain nationalised visions. To what extent the presentation of the capital remains authentic (as opposed to celluloid) is now of little consequence, because 'Korean-ness' is always present in the space, regardless of how it manifests itself. The production of *Parasite* is indicative of this. Unlike many of the other films discussed in the previous chapters of this book, which were all shot on location, *Parasite* features two Seoul residences that are entirely constructed—they were designed and built exclusively for the film (Jung 2020). This includes both the Park family's expansive, angular and ultra-modern house and the Kim family's basement flat, or 'Banjiha', as it is known in Korean (as well as the street on which it is located). While both settings are highly different, they are *equally* Korean and are primarily used to emphasise class tensions. The two settings illuminate the hybridised structure of Seoul and, by extension, the vast socio-economic polarity that exists amongst its residents. Thus, even though the physical appearance of Seoul in *Parasite* is, on a literal level, manufactured, it is by no means an imagined space. Crucially, it still draws attention to specific national concerns and local issues.

Nevertheless, the fact that *Parasite's* primary landscapes are set designs or constructed 'stages' may, to some, be symptomatic of the growing, postmodern artificiality of the metropolis and, indeed, of Seoul. If the broad impression of South Korea's capital city can be so easily reproduced, it is entirely possible to question whether it still sustains any level of physical, cultural or national distinctiveness. However, this assumption disregards the history and development of Seoul, both on the cinema screen and in 'real' life, as well as its pivotal role in establishing South Korean cinema as a leading, national export. One can also argue that the ease with which it can be replicated, designed or 'built' on screen demonstrates the extent to which Seoul has become a recognisable, ubiquitous and, above all else, *Korean* product. Essentially, the unique spaces of the metropolis are so specific and nationally idiosyncratic that they can now be recreated as celluloid landscapes and thus provide a space (albeit a theatrical one) in which to convey not only a heightened realism but also a concentrated presentation of the Korean experience on screen. This is ultimately how the two residences in *Parasite* operate. They are used to convey the radical changes that have occurred across the city and, from a critical perspective, show how 'urban development and restructuring' continues to 'shape social inequality and exclusion' (Yang 2018, p. 3405). Whilst Korean film seeks to continuously focalise the capital city (and nationalise itself in the process), this does not necessarily mean that it seeks to manifest an idealistic or celebratory portrait of the urban landscape. Authentic representation of national space does, after all, rely on the conclusive acknowledgement of both the good and the bad.

What is especially unique about *Parasite*, however, is the way in which this criticism is presented and/or addressed by the sociopolitical narrative. The film follows the poor Kim family, who disguise themselves as common service workers in order to infiltrate the wealthy Park Household. When they eventually integrate themselves, both emotionally and physically, into the lives of the Park family, the Kims grow ever more resentful of their wealthier counterparts and disillusioned by their own, destitute circumstances. As with other Bong Joon Ho productions, the narrative inevitably changes direction in several surprising ways, but our emotional investment in the characters does not alter—if anything, it becomes more intense as the film progresses. This reaction is unexpected, particularly when the morality and general likeability of both families are called into question. In retrospect, however, this specific approach to characterisation is used as a device to further illuminate the more pressing social issues that occupy the heart of the narrative. Rather than blame the characters or families in the story (all of whom make very questionable decisions), the film draws attention to the flaws and failings of the wider systems and structures in which these individuals live and co-exist.

There are no explicitly 'bad' characters or antagonists at whom we can direct our anger and dismay. This notion can also be applied to the title itself, as it is never quite clear who can be labelled as the 'parasite' of the story. Instead, any feelings of discontent are both a by-product of, and directed primarily towards, the urban settings and residences that the two families occupy (as well as the Korean social narratives they represent). As a consequence, the houses themselves adopt anthropomorphic qualities—they are by no means static or passive objects. The architecture of each setting reflects both the movement of the characters that reside within it and, by extension, the movement of the nation as a whole (Nas and Brakus 2004). The Kim household is chaotic, disorderly and cramped, but ultimately a warm space (in the sense that the characters share a close bond). The Park family, meanwhile, are distant and emotionally stilted—they are as constrained and formal as the minimalistic walls that surround them. Essentially, all the characters in *Parasite* act as symbolic extensions of both their urban environment and class difference. And even though this presentation can be far from subtle, it is more importantly used to directly address the pressing social and economic issues, as well as the stark class polarity, that continue to exist within contemporary South Korean society. This also demonstrates how examples of national cinema need not share any commonality with the government or other ruling institutions—they can instead manifest and promote clear narratives of resistance (and in turn mobilise the viewing public and the collective national imagination in a highly specific way).

Nevertheless, the story in *Parasite* is not the only nationalising component of the film. More so than any other of Bong Joon Ho's works, *Parasite* contains highly deliberate allusions and visual parallels to other South Korean cinematic texts, which suggests it should be read as part of a much broader, yet constantly evolving, cultural timeline. There are, for example, continual references to stairs within the film. Whether separating the transgressive spaces of the Park household or emphasising the long urban descent to the Kim's basement apartment, the once menial function of the prosaic staircase is transformed into a visual tool of strong critique—something that was once perhaps more famously associated with Kim Ki-Young's *The Housemaid* (1960). Elsewhere, the presentation of Seoul city as a site burdened by both temporal and spatial *levels* of conflict bears a striking resemblance to the city seen within Park Kwang-Su's *Chilsu and Mansu* (1988), in which obstructive urban architecture quite literally halts any communication between the social classes. In these instances, *Parasite* is deliberately consolidating pre-existing feats of South Korean cinema and using such parallels to further its own national cause. I would therefore argue that *Parasite* acts as the inaugural text of a new 'Golden Age' in South Korean cinema. It brings to stylistic fruition and acknowledges a number of the country's historic cinematic movements, narratives and agendas.

Elsewhere, the emphasis on urban existence (and the presentation of, and engagement with, the city as a fundamentally sensory experience) has remained a consistent feature in many South Korean post-millennial cinematic productions, including the ones discussed throughout this book. When considering South Korea's turbulent history, a focus on the urban landscape may be regarded as a thematic priority because it is often assumed that the city is a space that fosters progress and stimulates cultural and national awareness. Essentially, the depiction of Seoul on screen has provided a necessary framework in which to explore the development of the Korean social landscape and, more importantly, relocate and/or redefine the concept of the Korean 'self'. Collectively, these consistent approaches to specific cultural and social concerns are what have allowed South Korean cinema, in the post-millennial age, to move beyond the limitations of the transnational and, instead, secure a place at the *centre of the national*.

Final Word

In the age of globalisation and modernisation, it is easy to dismiss Seoul as nothing more than a hyper-urban archetype, expanding and advancing in a manner that is not entirely dissimilar to other national cities. As Soochul Kim argues, 'the newly fashioned consumption spaces in Seoul seems to shock urban inhabitants by bombarding Seoulites with a variety of stimuli and a dizzy array of representations' (Kim 2009, p. 256). While this may, to a certain extent, be true (especially when considering the country's exponential economic development and global cultural pursuits), the persistent recognition it has received on film and, indeed, in other modes of popular culture suggests that Seoul still represents and reflects the core characteristics of South Korean national consciousness. Alongside the Korean people, the capital city has adapted and evolved—it is synonymous with the country's profound national transformation. Therefore, it cannot be regarded as a homogeneous, postmodern space. To label it as such significantly undermines the inter-generational and multifaceted disposition of its Korean residents.

Furthermore, Seoul has witnessed, and been significantly shaped by, systemic periods of destruction and renewal, which means its structural hybridity is important not only to the formation of South Korea's present, contemporary image but also to the preservation of its historical identity. As Baek Jin observes, 'the eruption of diversity in Korean architecture [within the cityscape] reflects the dramatic sense of emancipation upon the dissolution of authoritarian regimes' (Jin 2012, p. 58). For a country that, historically, has been denied the right to pursue and ultimately manifest its own autonomy and identity, this is highly important. There is a sense of an unparalleled Korean ownership of the capital and a level of national control that, for many years, had remained elusive to the Korean people. Thus, Seoul's development is symptomatic of the freedom South Korean society has experienced from the late Twentieth century to the present day. It continues to provide a shared, cathartic space in which the complex narratives of trauma and memory can be effectively visualised and, by extension, accepted (but by no means forgotten). Buildings are not simply concrete facades, but they offer 'rich, formal and spatial experiences' (Jin 2012, p. 58). Many of the characters discussed within this book are moulded by the transformative nature of the cityscape and the ceremonious 'experiences' to which Baek Jin refers. The Korean 'self', and its manifestation on film, can always be read in terms of its relationship to, and connection with, the urban environment. Whether it be Tae-Suk and Sun-Hwa on their urban quest for self-validation and fulfilment in *3-Iron*, or Tae-Sik's ruthless search for redemption in *The Man from Nowhere*, the backdrop of cinematic Seoul has continued to provide companionship to the most complex protagonists of post-millennial South Korean film. And while the presentation of the cityscape in such texts will remain, to some degree, celluloid, there will always be recognisable cultural elements, fragments of 'Korean-ness' and deep national truths embedded within.

References

Jin, B. 2012. Redefining Regionalism: Politics, Tradition and Identity in Korean Architecture. In *Convergent Flux: Architecture and Urbanism in Korea*, ed. Jinhee Park and John Hong, 56–89. Basel: Birkhauser.

Joo, J. 2010. Setting the Scene for the Boom: The Korean Government's Policies and the Resurgence of the Korean Film Industry. *The Journal of Asia-Pacific Studies* 17 (3): 151–167.

Jung, E. 2020. The House that Parasite Built (From Scratch) or How Bong Joon Ho Built the Houses in Parasite. *Vulture*. Accessed 29 September 2020. https://www.vulture.com/2020/02/how-bong-joon-ho-built-the-houses-in-parasite.html.

Kim, S. 2009. Re-locating the National: Spatialization of the National Past in Seoul. *Policy Futures in Education* 7 (2): 256–265. https://doi.org/10.2304/pfie.2009.7.2.256.

Nas, P., and C. Brakus. 2004. Bricks of Movement: A Note on Anthropomorphic Architecture. *Space & Culture* 7 (3): 260–264.

Rose, S. 2020. American Horror Story: How the US Lost its Grip on Pop Culture. *The Guardian*. Accessed 4 October 2020. https://www.theguardian.com/culture/2020/sep/12/american-horror-story-how-the-us-lost-its-grip-on-pop-culture.

Ruiz, M. 2020. Everything We Know About the Parasite HBO Series. *Vogue*. Accessed 7 September 2020. https://www.vogue.com/article/parasite-tv-show-hbo-news-cast-date-trailer.

Yang, M. 2018. The Rise of Gangnam Style: Manufacturing the Urban Middle Class in Seoul, 1976–1996. *Urban Studies* 55 (15): 3404–3420. https://doi.org/10.1177/0042098017748092.

Filmography

Beineix, Jean-Jacques, dir., *Diva* (Les Films Galaxie, 1981).
Besson, Luc, dir., *Leon: The Professional* (Gaumont Buena Vista International, 1994).
Bong, Joon-Ho, dir., *Memories of Murder* (CJ Entertainment, 2003).
———, dir., *The Host* (Showbox Entertainment, 2006).
———, dir., *Mother* (CJ Entertainment, 2009).
———, dir., *Snowpiercer* (The Weinstein Company, 2013).
———, dir., *Okja* (Netflix, 2017).
———, dir., *Parasite* (CJ Entertainment, 2019).
Hwang, In-Ho, dir., *Spellbound* (CJ Entertainment, 2011).
Jeong, Jae-Eun, dir., *Take Care of My Cat* (Cinema Service, 2001).
Kang, Je-Gyu, dir., *Shiri* (CJ Entertainment, 1999).
Kim, Ki-Young, dir., *The Housemaid* (Kuk Dong, Seki Trading Company, 1960).
Kim, Ki-Duk, dir., *3-Iron* (Cineclick Asia, 2004).
Kim, Bora, dir., *House of Hummingbird* (Epiphany Film, 2018).
Kwak, Jae-Yong, dir., *My Sassy Girl* (Cinema Service, 2001).
Lee, Chang-Dong, dir., *Oasis* (CJ Entertainment, 2002).
———, dir., *Secret Sunshine* (Cinema Service, 2007).
———, dir., *Poetry* (Next Entertainment World, 2010a).
Lee, Kyoung-Mi, dir., *Crush and Blush* (Vantage Holdings, 2008).
Lee, Jeong-Beom, dir., *The Man from Nowhere* (CJ Entertainment, 2010b).
Lee, Spike, dir., *Oldboy* (FilmDistrict, 2013).
Mann, Michael, dir., *Heat* (Warner Bros., 1995).
Morel, Pierre, dir., *Taken* (20th Century Fox, 2008).

© The Author(s), under exclusive license to Springer Nature Switzerland AG 2023
G. Ballard, *Urban Landscapes and National Visions in Post-Millennial South Korean Cinema*, East Asian Popular Culture, https://doi.org/10.1007/978-3-031-29739-7

Park, Ki-Hyung, dir., *Whispering Corridors* (Cinema Service, 1998).
Park, Kwang-Su, dir., *Chilsu and Mansu* (Dong-a Exports Company, 1988).
Park, Chan-Wook, dir., *Oldboy* (Show East, 2003).
Park, Chan-Ok, dir., *Paju* (Warner Bros. Korea, 2009).
Shin, Jung-Won, dir., *Chaw* (Lotte Entertainment, 2009).
———, dir., *Ghost Sweepers* (Next Entertainment World, 2012).
Stahelski, Chad, dir., *John Wick* (Lionsgate, 2014).
Yeon, Sang-Ho, dir., *Train to Busan* (Next Entertainment World, 2016).
Yim, Soon-Rye, *Forever the Moment* (Sidus FNH, 2008).
Yu, Hyun-Mok, dir., *Obaltan* (Cinema Epoch, 1960).

Index

A
Americanisation, 142, 144, 148
 TV adaptations, 160
America on screen
 urban anonymity, 69
Anti-American sentiment, 147, 149

B
Binaries, 143, 154
 Korea *vs* America, 148
 nature *vs* civilisation, 151
A Bittersweet Life, 86
Blockbuster
 cinematic difference, 70
 as Hollywood product, 43, 47, 48
 as Korean product, 46, 49, 54, 61, 62
 as transnational product, 48, 51
Bong Joon Ho, 37
 genre subversion, 122
 Korean auteur, 3
Box office, 44, 51, 59
Busan, 16, 61, 83

C
Celluloid city, 10, 126, 136
Censorship, 76, 78
Character
 the anti-hero, 93
 the expendable woman, 116
 as extension of the urban environment, 163
 the gangster figure, 92
 as Korean construction, 63
 as representative figure, 62, 70, 87
Chaw, 57
Chilsu and Mansu, 116, 163
Chinese
 East Asian Cinema, 4
Cinematic violence, 81
 extreme cinema, 101
 the male body, 82, 99
Cinephilia, 50, 69
The city, 13, 30, 64
Cityscape, 8, 13, 18
The Coachman, 78
Colonial history, 10

Commerical Korean cinema, 143
  narrative causality, 149
Confucianism, 74, 77, 94, 96, 98, 114, 120, 130
Constructed history, 131
Crush and Blush, 112
Cultural production, 9

D
Daegu, 16, 83
Defamiliarisation, 59, 92
Diegesis, 28, 35, 54, 65, 95, 104, 129
  and female subjectivity, 134, 136
  and stylised space, 147
Difference, 15, 154
Diva (1981), 28
Domestic audience, 56, 71
  box office, 38

E
East Asian Cinema, 4, 5, 10, 37, 132
Economy
  South Korea, 68

F
False narratives, 157
Fan culture, 111
  fan service and social media, 111
Female adulthood, 121
Female experience, 112, 123, 131
Female identity
  'Korean-ness,' 131
  marginalisation, 96, 113
  patriarchal expectation, 119
  representation, 114, 124
  transgression, 115
  visibility, 117
  voice, 123, 124

Film categorisation, 40, 67, 141
  art cinema, 122
Film noir, 116
  The Housemaid, 116
Film studies, 8
  and comparative approaches, 159
  and national approaches, 144, 154
  reader and text, 56, 70
Forever the Moment, 112

G
Gender bias, 109
  gendered histories, 118
Gender relations, 96
  gendered space, 115
  hegemony, 98, 113
  industry practice, 110
  patriarchal control, 115, 124
Genre, 6, 22, 49, 52, 67
  conventions, 56
  experimentation, 153
  the gangster film, 80, 81, 83, 84, 87, 90
  hybridity, 105, 113
  Korean monster blockbuster, 59
  and liminal film space, 123, 134
  and semiotic approaches, 49
  the Seoul Genre, 70
  Take Care of My Cat, 121
Ghost Sweepers, 57
Girlhood, 132, 134, 135
Globalisation, 5, 69, 80, 90, 104, 142, 146
The Golden Age, 75, 78, 113, 163

H
Hallyu, 2, 111
Han River, 53, 62, 149
Hollywood cinema, 5, 30, 61, 67, 81, 84, 90, 91, 160
  cinematic dominance, 37, 71, 85

Hong Kong cinema
  East Asian Cinema, 4
The Host, 53, 143, 149
The Housemaid, 113, 120
House of Hummingbird, 126
Hybridisation, 22, 30, 50, 123, 146, 152
  identity, 36
  intertextuality, 57

I

Imagined space, 15, 65
Incheon, 16
Take Care of My Cat, 124

J

Japanese cinema
  East Asian Cinema, 4
Jeong Jae-Eun, 124, 126
John Wick, 90

K

Kim Bora, 126
Kim Ki Duk, 23, 29, 38
Korean/American co-production, 141
Korean auteur
  Bong Joon Ho, 109, 141, 148
  Hong Sangsoo, 109
  Kim Jee-Woon, 109
  Kim Ki-Duk, 109
  Lee Chang-Dong, 109
  Park Chan Wook, 109
Korean film industry, 38, 53, 60, 67, 71, 79, 86, 92, 110, 119, 143
  and global practices, 144
  production to exhibition, 51
  as a self-governed institution, 160
Korean horror cinema, 57, 132, 133

Korean hostess films, 117
Korean new wave, 71
Korean popular culture, 112
  global response, 121, 141

L

Leon: The Professional, 90
Localisation, 44, 59, 147
  cultural specificity, 52

M

The Man from Nowhere, 87, 102
Mann, Michael, 84
Masculine identity, 73, 79, 105
  Korean military, 66, 74
  masculinity and nationhood, 73
  soldierly masculinity, 75, 100
  tradition and modernity, 118
Masculine narratives, 109, 110, 117
  Confucianism, 74
  the gangster figure, 83
  male anxiety, 114
  male crisis, 93, 97
  male ownership, 115, 123
  the male subject and national identity, 109
  male trauma, 77, 79
  patriarchy, 74, 75, 85, 92, 130
  post-war masculinity, 76
  and urban identity, 84
Masculinity
  desire, 85
  the 'father figure,' 97
Memories of Murder, 143
Mise-en-scene, 89, 104
Modernisation, 117
Mother, 143
Mythologisation, 18, 26, 125
  national narrative, 130

N

National audience, 44
National cinema, 6, 26, 67, 80, 85, 87
National identity, 7, 15, 26, 56, 60, 64, 109, 117
   cultural and historical, 52, 66
   nationhood and duty, 130
   post-authoritarian image, 160
National image, 21, 55
Nationalisation, 49, 60, 64
Nationalism, 25
National specificity, 142
National trauma, 80, 82
New York City, 147, 149
North Korea
   cinematic representation, 46

O

Oasis, 110
Obaltan, 76, 84, 88, 99
Okja, 141
Oldboy, 86, 90, 116
   American version, 91
Orientalism, 2
Oscars, 1
Otherness, 5, 38, 101, 150, 155
   non-Korean narratives, 128
Over-centralisation
   Seoul, 9

P

Paju, 112
Pansori, 118
   cultural heritage, 117
Parasite, 2, 5, 110, 154, 159–161
Park Chan Wook, 37
Performativity
   simulations, 147
Poetry, 110
Popular film discourse, 90, 149

Postmodernity, 14, 18, 27, 30
   as cinematic style, 66
Post-war society, 78
Psycho-geography
   the city and the individual, 18

R

Remasculinization
   Kyung Hyun Kim, 86, 93, 94
Romance Papa, 78

S

Scorsese, Martin, 84
Secret Sunshine, 110
The self, 27, 31, 60, 164
   identity construction, 33
Seoul city, 9, 10
   as authentic landscape, 68, 150
   as binary space, 145
   construction, 18, 58, 88, 146
   as extension of female experience, 125
   as lived experience, 104
   modernisation and globalisation, 15, 59
   national identity, 16, 156, 164
   as national paradigm, 63, 162
   national representation, 17, 46, 54
   and the natural environment, 146
   real and imagined, 21, 55, 60, 64, 69, 94, 161
   as working realm, 151
Seoulite, 18, 27, 55, 58, 94, 150, 164
Separateness, 143
Shiri, 43
Snowpiercer, 142
Soft power, 81
Soja, Edward
   Spatial Trialectics, 20
   Thirdspace, 21, 64

Sonyeo sensibility, 133
Sopyeonje, 116, 117, 119, 120
Space and place, 19, 30
Spellbound, 57
Stairs in Korean cinema, 163
Subjectivity, 102, 116, 126, 150
 Jacques Lacan, 33
 mirroring, 28
Sunshine Policy, 45

T
Take Care of My Cat, 111, 120, 132, 136
A Tale of Two Sisters, 133
A Tender Heart, 78
Thirdspace, 20, 32
 Homi Bhabha, 22
Thirst, 101
3-Iron, 23, 37
The touristic gaze, 68, 125
Train to Busan, 56
Trans-historical approaches, 86
Transnationalism, 6, 156
 film practice, 152
 global desires, 128, 137

U
Unconventionality
 genre subversion, 91, 92
Urban, 20
 condition, 34, 164
 gendered perspectives, 126
 modernisation, 13
 narrative, 23
 as nationally specific, 100
 space, 14, 30, 54, 58, 64, 83
 stereotypes, 145

W
The Wailing, 101
Whispering Corridors, 132
Women directors, 112, 122
Women's cinema, 111, 119
 industry practice, 110, 136
Women's narratives
 duty and desire, 128
 foreign longing, 138

Y
Yakuza, 87